Talking about Terrorism

Responding to Children's Questions

For our families, especially Nigel and Chris

Also written by Alison Jamieson and Jane Flint:
Radicalisation and Terrorism: A Teacher's Handbook for Addressing Extremism

Published by Brilliant Publications Limited
Unit 10
Sparrow Hall Farm
Edlesborough
Dunstable
Bedfordshire
LU6 2ES, UK

Website: www.brilliantpublications.co.uk

Written by Alison Jamieson and Jane Flint
Edited by Marie Birkinshaw
Photo research by Susannah Jayes
Illustrated by Kerry Ingham
Cover by Gaynor Berry

Printed ISBN: 978-1-78317-278-8
ebook ISBN: 978-1-78317-279-5

First printed and published in the UK in 2017.

The poem 'If mice could roar' from *Ruskin Bond's Book of Verse*, Penguin Books India (2007) has been reprinted with the generous permission of Ruskin Bond and Penguin Books India.

Photo credits:
p 11: Alamy/Stacy Walsh Rosenstock
p 29: Getty Images/Daniel Munoz
p 35 top: UK Safer Internet Centre; bottom: Alamy/dpt picture alliance
p 37: Shutterstock/ Leah-Anne Thompson
p 39: REX Shutterstock
p 40 left: Shutterstock/pattang; right: Shutterstock/Stuart G Porter
p 41 left: Shutterstock/ntdanai; right: Shutterstock/Wead
p 48 Alamy/Newzulu
p 52 top left: Getty Images/Ullstein Bild; top right: Metropolitan Museum of Art, New York; bottom left: iStockphoto/golibo; bottom right: Getty Images/Hulton-Deutsch Collection/Corbis
p 53 top left: Alamy/Granger Historical Picture Archive; top centre: Alamy/Everett Collection Historical; top right: Alamy/Allstar Picture Library; bottom left: Alamy/REUTERS; bottom right: Alamy/REUTERS
p 58: Hertfordshire Constabulary
p 59: Shutterstock/Debu55y
p 65 left: Shutterstock/John Gomez; centre left: Shutterstock/Zurijeta; centre right: Getty Images/Shaun Curry/AFP; right: Shutterstock/g-stockstudio
p 69: Alamy/Greatstock
p 71: Shutterstock/Maykherkevych
p 81: Shutterstock/jeff gynane
p 82 top: Alamy/Granger Historical Picture Archive; bottom: Alamy/Everett Collection Historical
p 85: Alamy/Xinhua
p 86 left: Getty Images/Ian Nicholson/WPA Pool; right: Alamy/WENN Ltd
p 87: Alamy/Michael Debets
p 88: Metropolitan Museum of Art, New York
p 89: Alamy/Photo Researchers, Inc
p 90: Alamy/Mark Kerrison
p 93: iStockphoto/jcarillet
p 95: Getty Images/Walter Dhladhla/AFP
p 98: Alison Jamieson
p 109: iStockphoto/jcarillet

Talking about Terrorism

Responding to Children's Questions

Alison Jamieson and
Jane Flint

with

Foreword by Peter Wanless, Chief Executive, NSPCC

Message from the Jo Cox Foundation

Foreword

In today's world barely a week goes by without us hearing of yet another atrocious terrorist attack. These are uncertain times and, for children, it can be incredibly upsetting for them to see and hear such violence happening both at home and abroad.

Following the devastating Paris attacks in 2015 the NSPCC's Childline service received hundreds of calls from frightened young people who were seeking reassurance and answers. Even now we still hear from children who are petrified about what is going on around them and fear that they or their loved ones could be hurt by terrorists.

Terrorism is a difficult and complex issue but it must be confronted head on. For this to happen children need to be able to talk openly about it and know how to stay safe from anyone who may attempt to radicalise them for dangerous acts.

Teachers are well placed to have these challenging conversations with young people. They can explain what terrorism is and how people are tricked into joining terrorist groups. They can reassure them that there is a lot of goodness in the world, and explain why it is crucial that we celebrate one another's differences and cultures.

If we are to reassure our young people, encourage their tolerance of others, and prevent them from being groomed into acts that could hurt themselves or others, we must talk with them and educate them. This book sets out to help teachers do just that.

The Internet and 24-hour news cycle means that it is impossible to shield children from the reality of terrorist attacks. But, with open conversation and clear explanations, we can help them feel safe and know that the world is still a good place.

Peter Wanless
Chief Executive, NSPCC

Message from the Jo Cox Foundation

The world today is witnessing huge political and cultural shifts – one of these is the rise of extremism. Extremism in all its forms presents those working with children and young people with the challenge of how to have responsible, honest and caring conversations with children.

Long before the act of hatred that took Jo Cox from us, Jo was concerned about what was happening to tolerance in our world. Acts of extremism and hate are designed to divide us but Jo believed we are stronger when we unite around the things that we hold in common.

Jo spent a lot of her time as an MP in schools in her home constituency of Yorkshire talking about her vision for a fairer, kinder and more tolerant world. These values are only as strong as the foundations underlying them and the scaffolding that we create. Jo believed that values and beliefs are shaped from the youngest age – children and young people can and should be equipped with the confidence to stand up for these values.

Jo really did live by the conviction that we have 'more in common than that which divides us.' As this book also shows, it is this phrase that can and should guide conversations with children about extremism in all its forms.

Iona Lawrence
Director, Jo Cox Foundation

Preface

Teaching professionals in Britain today face unprecedented challenges, of which the new safeguarding responsibilities with regard to terrorism are among the most demanding. Many teachers are uncertain about what is being asked of them, about how they should respond to questions about terrorism and how, or if, they should address extremist ideologies in the classroom.

Children's questions about terrorism and how to answer them was the starting point for the collaboration between Jane Flint and myself, and led to the publication of our Key Stage 3 teachers' resource, *Radicalisation and Terrorism: A Teacher's Handbook for Addressing Extremism*, in 2015. The enthusiastic response from teachers to the Handbook, followed by requests for special needs and primary level texts, encouraged us to proceed with *Talking about Terrorism*.

In fact, we had long believed that a separate resource text was needed for Key Stage 2, also intended for classroom use but with a simple question and answer format that would reflect children's concerns directly. Jane's experience of teaching in a primary school in Beeston, Leeds, at the time of the London transport bombings in 2005 had convinced us of this. As first responder in her classroom on the day of the attacks, she struggled without resources to cope with the questions put by her pupils: 'What do the terrorists want?', 'Why are they so angry?', and 'When will the next attack happen?' In the days that followed, the demands made of her and her colleagues multiplied. The children's anxieties deepened with news that three of the suicide bombers were from or had connections to Beeston, and that one had been a well-liked teaching assistant in a local primary school. Her school's many Muslim pupils required particularly sensitive care to protect them from victimisation as a small but vocal sector of the local community began an organised campaign of anti-Muslim hostility and abuse. Attempts to sow division and hatred within the community continued long afterwards.

In the confusion that inevitably follows a terrorist attack, adults search for the right words to reassure and to explain, but they can be hard to find. Many teachers feel they lack the skills to engage in open classroom discussion, relying instead on video clips made for children's TV or on occasional visits from police *Prevent* officers. While these can be valuable they are no substitute for meaningful dialogue between pupils and a trusted teacher.

Until now, there have been no resource texts about terrorism specifically dedicated to the Key Stage 2 age group. Existing school resources tend to focus on older age groups on the assumption that primary classes should be protected from unpleasant or difficult subjects, and that the issues are beyond their comprehension. We disagree. In our view it is precisely this age group that is most in need of simple, straightforward explanations. Younger children may be more anxious because of fears they cannot express verbally and more vulnerable to prejudice and manipulative influences because they lack the skills to resist them. We believe that these are the children who can benefit most from the information that this book provides.

We have written *Talking about Terrorism* to support teachers and school leadership teams in meeting their new challenges. We believe that our unique combination of experiences – of primary school teaching on the one hand and years of studying terrorists and terrorism on the other – will give teachers the confidence to tackle controversial issues in the classroom, to respond to children's questions and to fulfil their statutory responsibilities.

Alison Jamieson

Contents

When? 88

All questions and answers are suitable for both Lower and Upper Key Stage 2 pupils, unless indicated for suitability for Upper Key Stage 2 only .

The smiley symbol indicates questions and answers with a particularly positive approach.

Introduction

Since the London transport bombings of 2005, Britain has been spared the type of mass casualty attacks seen in continental Europe, although the official terror threat level has been ‘severe’ since mid-2014, meaning that an attack is considered ‘highly likely’. On 22nd March 2017, shortly before this book went to press, a 52-year-old British man drove a vehicle into pedestrians on the pavement of Westminster Bridge in London, killing three and injuring many others. A fourth died later of her injuries. The man then crashed the vehicle into the railings around the Palace of Westminster and entered the Palace grounds, where he fatally stabbed an unarmed police officer. Although widely assumed to be an Islamist-inspired terrorist attack, the facts were unclear at time of writing. Thousands of Londoners attended a vigil in Trafalgar Square the same evening to reject violence and show solidarity with the dead and injured, while the work of Parliament continued as normal the following day after tributes to the victims.

While the principal terrorist threat is perceived to come from Islamist groups, other forms of violent extremism are sometimes overlooked. Although predominantly peaceful, Northern Ireland experienced 22 terrorist attacks in 2014 and 15 in 2015. Of growing concern is extreme right-wing violence, frequently in the form of hate crimes against foreigners or ethnic and religious minorities. This can be more difficult to prevent since it is often carried out by individuals or ‘lone wolves’ who operate below the radar of police and intelligence monitoring. One such individual, described as a terrorist by prosecutors, murdered Labour MP Jo Cox in June 2016 out of hatred for her compassionate policies towards refugees.

11 September 2001, the attack on the World Trade Center, New York

As well as increasing in frequency worldwide, terrorist attacks have acquired greater immediacy thanks to 24-hour news coverage and the availability of instant messaging and video-sharing on social media. A combination of the sheer quantity of news with the graphic quality of its imagery means that even the most watchful parents struggle to protect their children entirely from exposure to terrorism. Shocking images, even fleetingly glimpsed, can be mesmerising and etched indelibly in children’s memories. Their perceptions of violent events may be unexpected, and vary significantly from those of adults. They may find ‘magical explanations’ of their own invention or become fixated with a single image, such as a pet abandoned in a bombed-out building or a seabird trapped in an oilslick. After the 9/11 attacks in New York in 2001, some children believed that dozens of planes had crashed into the Twin Towers because the video footage was repeatedly replayed on TV.[1]

Children's responses to terrorism are direct and very personal: they worry about their homes, families and pets, and seek reassurance from adults that their world is safe and under control. Their reactions tend to mirror those of key adults around them, hence the advice generally given to parents and teachers to be as restrained as possible in their behaviour and speech, to keep calm and to maintain daily routines where possible.

Children also try to make broader sense of tragic events, asking searching questions that cannot be deflected with superficial responses. After the multiple terrorist attacks in Paris in November 2015 in which 130 died, British children as young as nine sought advice from the NSPCC's Childline. In the five months after the Paris attacks, Childline provided more than 400 counselling sessions to children who were frightened to leave home and fearful that similar attacks might happen in the UK. In France, the difficulties encountered by parents and teachers in explaining the attacks prompted journalists at a children's daily newspaper, *Le Petit Quotidien*, to produce a special issue which included answers to questions put to them by a group of 8-year-olds in a Paris classroom.

What this book is about

Talking about Terrorism is structured around 40 questions that children may ask (or, in our experience, have asked). We explain terrorism as a kind of jigsaw, made up of six key question lines:

Where?

Four principal aims of this book:

- ❖ to help teachers to answer children's questions about terrorism in a simple, direct and honest format
- ❖ to provide a reliable and comprehensive guide to the issues surrounding terrorist violence
- ❖ to assist in promoting creativity, understanding and critical thinking across the KS2 curriculum, including safe use of Internet and associated technologies
- ❖ to support teachers and school leadership teams in implementing their *Prevent* duties

The questions are phrased in the language that children use and answered using expressions and concepts with which they are familiar. We provide simple, objective explanations and try where possible to reassure, while being careful not to raise unrealistic expectations.

What the book offers, apart from questions and answers

The text is interspersed with activities that stimulate critical thinking and encourage creative investigation of our themes. These range from discussions and debates, the use of circle time and hot-seating through to role-play, poetry and music composition, singing and artwork. We constantly weave global concerns with children's everyday lives. A fictional Storyline narrates the human tragedy of conflict as told through the loss of a beloved teddy bear, whose return to his rightful owner becomes a symbol of hope and peace.

Global concerns are interwoven with children's everyday lives

Activities include discussions and debates, circle time and hot-seating, role-play, poetry and music composition, singing and artwork

We give particular importance to peacemaking and reconciliation and include examples of how conflict was resolved in Northern Ireland and South Africa. We describe how a peace process works, and how a compromise can be reached, usually after a long and difficult search for common ground. We explain the role of mediators and of peacemakers, individuals with special qualities whom we call 'Courageous People'. As we show, terrorism is not found in nature, it is man-made, and therefore 'man' can end it.

We emphasise peacemaking and reconciliation

Terrorism is man-made therefore 'man' can end it

Despite the focus on terrorism we never lose sight of a core belief in human goodness, and this emerges strongly from each of the principal sections. We make it a priority to focus on positive actions that children can perform, singly or collectively, to make the world more peaceful. Even in the worst situations we always find exceptional qualities of courage, generosity and kindness. We show how an off-duty police constable saved the lives of two of her fellow passengers on the London Tube in 2005, and illustrate the compassion and commitment to peace shown by the Pakistani teenager Malala Yousafzai after her shooting by the Taliban. We show how, after the Paris attacks of 2015, Parisians opened their homes to those stranded in the city, how volunteers queued for hours to donate blood and how taxi drivers drove the wounded home or to hospital without payment. We explain how ordinary people gathered together for a vigil were 'standing together' against terrorism, showing they were not afraid. Each section has inspiring stories of peacemaking and reconciliation, about the power of love over hate, of non-violence over violence and the importance of tolerance and respect.

Children can help to make the world more peaceful

Inspiring stories show the power of love over hate, of non-violence over violence and the importance of tolerance and respect

What we say about terrorism

We say that terrorism is 'violence that makes people afraid and upset'

We say that terrorism is 'violence that makes people afraid and upset', carried out by individuals who are angry and full of hate. At the simplest level we say terrorism is 'violence used for a reward' and give examples of the rewards that terrorists want. We use the idea of a terrorism 'cooking pot' in which we generally find certain ingredients. Unless we find these ingredients in the pot, what we're looking at probably isn't terrorism. We take the view that terrorism is a kind of war, usually started by a weaker group against a much stronger one. We consider that terrorism is always destructive, that it brings suffering and loss and almost never anything good. We try to explain what terrorism *is* in part by what it is *not*, and contrast it with other forms of violence – such as those found in nature and those that are man-made. Bullying is not terrorism, nor is bank robbery. While terrorists may act alone, their actions are generally claimed on behalf of a wider community.

We stress that terrorism is always a choice

We stress that terrorist violence is always a choice, made by each individual for different reasons. We cannot say that anything 'causes' terrorism or that there is a 'typical' terrorist. We explain that the choice can be influenced by different factors. We introduce 'push and pull' forces, namely experiences that push individuals away from what they view as a bad situation and ideas or beliefs that pull them towards something they think will be better. We show that fear can be a driving force in terrorism, and that, strange though it may seem, terrorists usually think *they* are the victims of aggression, and that they are rescuing or defending a community from oppression.

We explain terrorism as a social narrative

We explain terrorism as a social narrative, translated for children as a kind of storytelling. We introduce the idea of grievances or, for Lower KS2 pupils, strong feelings of anger, hatred and that 'things aren't fair': these are the elements that bind an individual to the story. The story can be true, made-up or exaggerated, and can change with time or under different influences. It can be passed between generations or between contemporaries. We explain that experiences of humiliation and being treated without respect are among the strongest grievances; that in a minority of people, these can lead to hatred and a desire to avenge perceived wrongs to themselves or to those with whom they identify. But we stress repeatedly that while grievances may be common to many, very few people become terrorists.

We examine why religion is often associated with terrorism. We stress that although religion is used to 'justify' violence, terrorist leaders often twist religious writings to make people follow them and to compel obedience.

We use the expression ‘in the name of’ a religion when we explain religious-inspired terrorism. This is in order to mark a distance from what religious teachings say and how terrorists have used them. Our message is, ‘People use violence “in the name of” religion but they’ve misunderstood, they’ve got the story wrong’. We also provide examples of different kinds of terrorism that have nothing to do with religion.

We examine why religion is often associated with terrorism

We do not pretend that Britain can be fully protected from terrorist attack. In our view, to imply this would be unwise in the current climate, but we minimise the dangers where possible. We stress that Britain’s strict laws and island status make it an extremely safe place to live, and that there are thousands of people working every day and night to keep us safe. Our view is that although children look for reassurance, they can also deal with uncertainty. They can accept that there are things that we simply do not know, and questions we cannot answer. We provide specific details of terrorist attacks to help teachers to explain a particular event, if asked, but they are at liberty to provide or withhold the information as they see fit.

We do not pretend that Britain can be fully protected from a terrorist attack

Curriculum links

Talking about Terrorism complements diverse parts of the KS2 curriculum within RE, History, PSHE, ICT and SMSC. The text can be used in **RE** to correct the common assumption that terrorism derives from religion. We stress the common values of all the main religions, and say that if killing civilians is being ‘justified’ and used ‘in the name of’ a religion, religious teaching is usually being twisted in a bad way. As regards the Key Concepts of the **History** curriculum, the text includes historically significant people and events (Julius Caesar, Guy Fawkes, the Suffragettes), uses historical terms such as empire (India under the British Empire) and explores social, cultural, religious and ethnic diversity in Britain and the wider world.

Within the **PSHE** curriculum the module *Living in the Wider World* is especially relevant. We encourage discussions about rights and responsibilities, diversity and equality and discrimination and prejudice, always connecting children’s experiences in the family, school and community to a wider framework. The Suffragettes could be included in PSHE studies of Parliament, democracy and how laws are made.

Talking about Terrorism draws on aspects of the **ICT** curriculum to encourage safe and responsible use of the Internet and associated technology. We devote particular attention to protecting pupils from being influenced by pro-violence messages via the Internet or social media. We believe that school strategies to disrupt and resist such influences will be enhanced if pupils are encouraged to develop their own counter-narratives, even at KS2 level. We invite them to reflect on how stories are told on the basis of *fact, fiction and opinion*, and ask them to think of ways to protect themselves from being tricked or misled by people or stories they might be inclined to believe.

Talking about Terrorism is as much about developing a set of core values as it is about terrorism, and can be used across the **Spiritual, Moral, Social and Cultural** curriculum. We examine the spiritual emptiness and quest for identity that some individuals seek to resolve through membership of a violent group. We reflect on the values and symbols shared by the world's major religions. We examine how terrorists try to justify the morality of using violence, portraying themselves as defenders rather than aggressors. We stress the need for respect and tolerance for different ways of thinking and living, provided that the rule of law is respected. We encourage children to explore their own and others' views, to practise moral decision-making and critical thinking. Children are invited to work in a team or in pairs to find ways of solving conflicts and resolving differences.

We study the nature of British values – what we consider to be the 'best of Britain' and explain how British democracy operates according to human rights and equality before the law. We look at decision- and law-making at national and international level, and at the freedom Britons have to engage in peaceful protest. We invite discussions of cultural development through the celebration of special events such as the Olympic and Paralympic games and through symbols of Britain's culture and diversity. We highlight the variety of accents and languages spoken across Britain and how words are adopted from other countries and continents. We reflect on the nature of identity and emphasise the common aspects of our identities that we share with others. We encourage the view of Britain as a hybrid, or crossover of traditions that have given us a love of diversity from cricket to curry to rap music. These bind us together and cross boundaries. We are aware of the high priority given to schools' development of SMSC by Ofsted, and are convinced that *Talking about Terrorism* can make a significant contribution in this regard.

Talking about Terrorism and Prevent

Since July 2015, education professionals have been placed on the front line of Britain's terrorism prevention efforts. The Counter-Terrorism and Security Act 2015 imposed the legal obligation on schools and other 'specified authorities' in the public sector to have 'due regard to the need to prevent people from being drawn into terrorism.'[2] This has added a broad range of statutory responsibilities to existing safeguarding duties. Schools must have in place 'mechanisms that enable staff to understand the risks of radicalisation, to recognise and respond appropriately and to be aware of how and where to find support.' After training, teachers should have 'the knowledge and confidence to identify children at risk of being drawn into terrorism and to challenge extremist ideas which can be used to legitimise terrorism and are shared by terrorist groups.' *Prevent* duty guidance recommends that schools be 'safe places where children and young people can understand and discuss sensitive topics, including terrorism and the extremist ideas that are part of terrorist ideology, and learn how to challenge these ideas.'[3]

In some respects the new safeguarding responsibilities under *Prevent* resemble those for protecting children from other harms in that they involve a partnership between schools, Local Safeguarding Children Boards, police, parents and local agencies or authorities. Individuals identified as vulnerable go before a dedicated panel, which may then recommend entry into a government deradicalisation programme known in England and Wales as *Channel*. (Scotland runs a separate deradicalisation programme, while *Prevent* does not apply in Northern Ireland.) Referral procedures are guided by a 'vulnerability assessment framework' consisting of 22 indicators spread over three categories. The criteria for perceived vulnerability depend on: *engagement* with an extremist group, cause or ideology, *intent* to use violence or other illegal means and *capability* to contribute directly or indirectly to an act of terrorism.[4]

Data provided by the National Police Chiefs' Council, the authority responsible for *Channel*, showed that almost four thousand referrals were made in England and Wales under the *Prevent* strategy in 2015, up from 1,681 in 2014. One third of these came from the education sector. Of the total, 54 per cent were under 18, with 1,424 referrals in the 11–15 age group and 414 aged 10 or younger.[5] Two thirds were male. Approximately two thirds of referrals related to Islamist extremism and 15 per cent to far-right extremism. As a result of the referrals made in 2015, 293 individuals, or around seven per cent of the total, had received 'supportive interventions' through *Channel*.

Prevent and the statutory duties it imposes across the public sector have been controversial, and teachers have reported insufficient training and uncertainty about their responsibilities. The measures are perceived by some as reflecting an anti-Muslim bias, and as carrying the risk of racial or religious profiling. The high number of referrals from schools has been interpreted as an over-reaction or misinterpretation by overzealous teaching staff and school leadership teams, fearful of the possible consequences of not acting pre-emptively. Some teachers feel that the obligation to watch for signs of radicalisation breaks the bond of trust between pupil and teacher and that it has effectively shut down the opportunities for school debates on controversial issues: that discussions are avoided at home and at school for fear that misreported conversations may be used as a basis of referral to *Channel*. Although the percentage of referrals requiring supportive interventions is low, this does not address the distress that may have been caused to individuals, schools and families by unnecessary referral.

We are not competent – nor is it the role of this book – to comment on the effectiveness of *Prevent* or on how the strategy has been delivered to schools. However we are convinced that the British government has a duty to support the education sector in safeguarding against indoctrination to violence, not least on account of the estimated 850 nationals, including children and young adults, who have left Britain to join Islamic State in Iraq and Syria.

For many young people, the quest to find an identity by identifying 'the other' as an enemy may appear the solution to an unfulfilled life. Just as hate, prejudice and stereotyping can be absorbed at an early age, we believe that encouraging values of respect, racial and gender equality and compassion through education can be a powerful counterforce. Our contribution, and we believe it is an important one, is to give educators the confidence to create the 'safe spaces' the government calls for, where pupils feel free to ask questions, explore answers and express their doubts and fears, and where choices can be openly debated. Indeed, we suggest that a significant number of *Prevent* referrals might be avoided if teachers were equipped with a better understanding of the issues around terrorism and radicalisation. Then, rather than going for the 'safe option' of a referral based on fear, greater knowledge would give them the confidence to make wiser assessments of risk and vulnerability.

Terminology and definitions

The range of definitions of terrorism, violent extremism and extremism used by scholars and by governments is extensive. Given the age group addressed, we do not discuss the terminology of terrorism in the text, but offer the following as general background. Use of the word **terrorism** is frequently subjective and value-laden, and attempts in the United Nations to find international consensus on a definition have repeatedly failed. Bruce Hoffman (2006) defines terrorism as 'the deliberate creation and exploitation of fear through violence or the threat of violence in the pursuit of political change.' Conor Gearty (1991) states, 'Violence is unequivocally terrorist when it is politically motivated and carried out by sub-state groups; when its victims are chosen at random; and when the purpose behind the violence is to communicate a message to a wider audience.' Section 1 of the UK Terrorism Act 2000 defines terrorism as 'the use or threat of action… [where] the use or threat is designed to influence the government or an international governmental organisation or to intimidate the public or a section of the public, and… is made for the purpose of advancing a political, religious, racial or ideological cause.'

Radicalisation is defined in the UK government's *Prevent* strategy 2011 as 'the process by which a person comes to support terrorism and forms of extremism leading to terrorism.' **Violent extremism**, according to *Prevent*, is 'the endorsement of violence to achieve extreme ends.' **Extremism** is defined as 'vocal or active opposition to fundamental British values, including democracy, the rule of law, individual liberty and mutual respect and tolerance of different faiths and beliefs.' While we agree that these values are British and are of paramount importance, we maintain they have a broader, universal significance that extends beyond British nationality and culture. We consider that extremist views are strong views that not many people share, or that not many people think are acceptable or correct. We do not believe that possessing such views is an indicator of support for, or participation in, terrorism.

In *Talking about Terrorism* we strip terrorism down to its simplest component parts. We say that terrorism is 'violence used for a reward' and that it is 'violence that makes people afraid and upset.' We say it is driven by anger, hatred, and a sense that wrong things have been done and not put right. We provide further 'ingredients' for a terrorism 'cooking pot' which can be introduced as appropriate.

How to get the most out of this book

Every section is optional and there is no obligatory reading or study order although we suggest that you begin with the What? questions as they lay the groundwork for understanding key words and themes mentioned later in the text. From this point you should select the questions and answers that you consider most appropriate – for your class, for the curriculum time available and for the theme of your chosen lesson. Your choice may be influenced by events in the news, or by a situation that has developed in your class or community. You may wish to concentrate on the optimistic stories of peacemaking and of activism by Courageous People. Describing the history of the peace bridge in Londonderry/Derry or the lives of Nelson Mandela and Malala Yousafzai could take precedence over understanding the influences that draw someone into terrorism.

We have deliberately created overlaps between the sections as regards the principal themes. The key concepts we use are anger, hatred and a sense

> *The key concepts we use are anger, hatred and a sense of unfairness or grievance*

of unfairness or grievance, and these words recur frequently, though different examples and different approaches are used. The aim is to provide continuity and avoid the need to search or cross-check as you address each question. We have differentiated the sections and activities as we consider appropriate for Lower and Upper KS2 but these should be adapted as appropriate to your class and school. All the questions we ask could be rephrased, and we encourage you to adapt and be flexible. For example the question, 'How does terrorism start?' could easily be 'Where does terrorism come from?' or 'Why does terrorism happen?'

We encourage you to move back and forth from situations based on local or personal experiences to global problems, and from present-day to historical examples. As you link individual actions to those of a wider community, and explore ideas of conflict and grievance, identity, human rights and democratic values you will show your pupils how their lives are interwoven with a much bigger society in which they are active participants, and which they themselves can influence and change.

What to look out for in each section

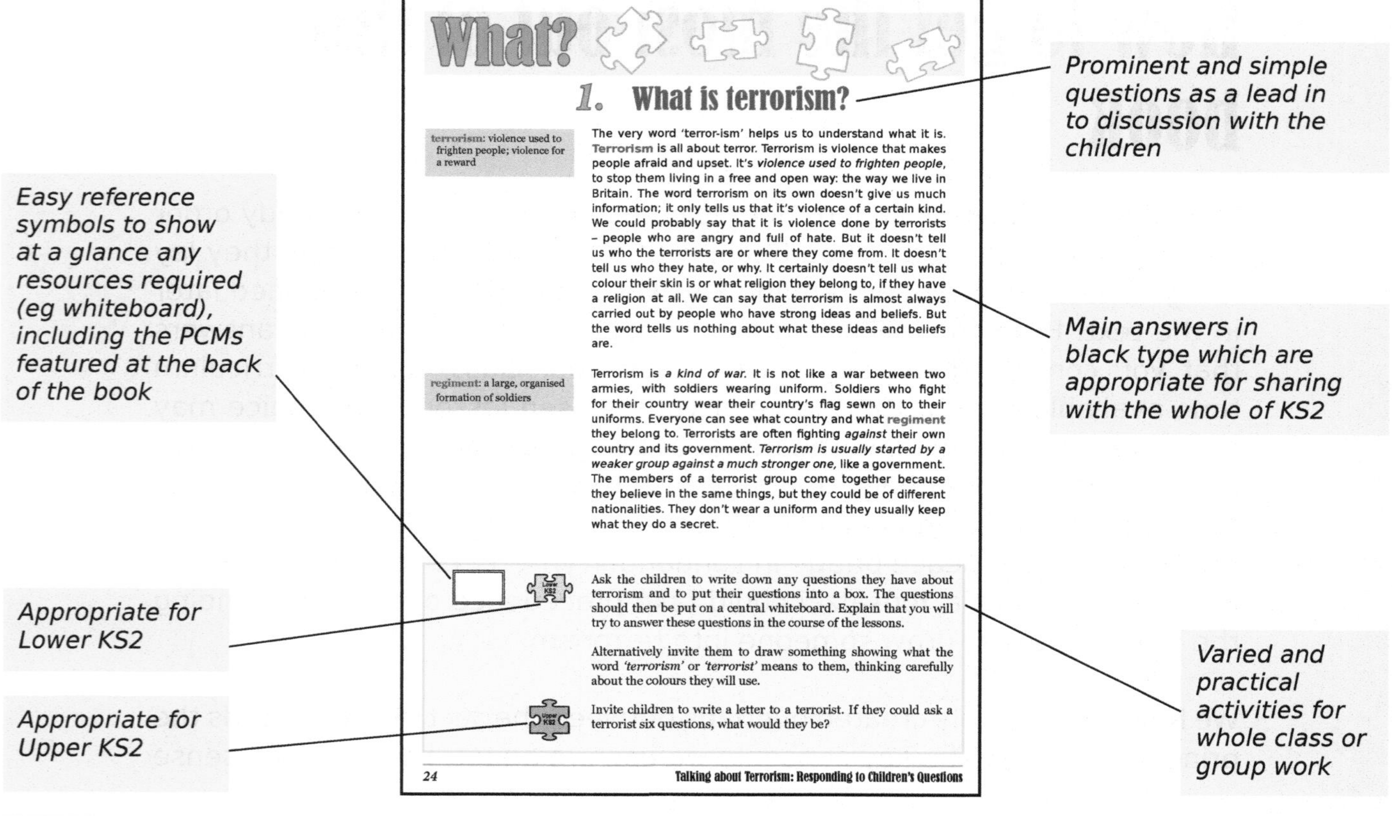

What?

1. What is terrorism?

terrorism: violence used to frighten people; violence for a reward

The very word 'terror-ism' helps us to understand what it is. **Terrorism** is all about terror. Terrorism is violence that makes people afraid and upset. It's *violence used to frighten people*, to stop them living in a free and open way: the way we live in Britain. The word terrorism on its own doesn't give us much information; it only tells us that it's violence of a certain kind. We could probably say that it is violence done by terrorists – people who are angry and full of hate. But it doesn't tell us who the terrorists are or where they come from. It doesn't tell us who they hate, or why. It certainly doesn't tell us what colour their skin is or what religion they belong to, if they have a religion at all. We can say that terrorism is almost always carried out by people who have strong ideas and beliefs. But the word tells us nothing about what these ideas and beliefs are.

regiment: a large, organised formation of soldiers

Terrorism is *a kind of war*. It is not like a war between two armies, with soldiers wearing uniform. Soldiers who fight for their country wear their country's flag sewn on to their uniforms. Everyone can see what country and what **regiment** they belong to. Terrorists are often fighting *against* their own country and its government. *Terrorism is usually started by a weaker group against a much stronger one*, like a government. The members of a terrorist group come together because they believe in the same things, but they could be of different nationalities. They don't wear a uniform and they usually keep what they do a secret.

Ask the children to write down any questions they have about terrorism and to put their questions into a box. The questions should then be put on a central whiteboard. Explain that you will try to answer these questions in the course of the lessons.

Alternatively invite them to draw something showing what the word *'terrorism'* or *'terrorist'* means to them, thinking carefully about the colours they will use.

Invite children to write a letter to a terrorist. If they could ask a terrorist six questions, what would they be?

24 Talking about Terrorism: Responding to Children's Questions

Where?

There were many protests about this, and some of them turned violent. Most Catholics in Northern Ireland wanted all of Ireland to be an independent country and not a part of Britain. Most Protestants wanted Northern Ireland to stay as a part of Britain. Catholic and Protestant terrorist groups were formed. The Provisional Irish Republican Army (the IRA) was formed in 1969. Its goal was to get rid of British rule in Northern Ireland. Its members thought that the only way to do this was by using violence. The British army was sent to Northern Ireland to keep order. The army also used violence, especially in Catholic areas. The IRA used terrorism against Protestant groups *and* against the British army.

Teacher's tip
If appropriate, explain that Catholics and Protestants are all Christians, but they follow Christianity in different ways. One difference is that Catholics consider the Pope to be head of the Church, whereas Protestants do not recognise his authority.

From 1969 till 1998 over 3,600 people were killed by bombs and guns. More than two thousand of them were ordinary men, women and children.

After many years the terrorist groups realised that neither side was going to win. The violence had brought great suffering to both the Catholic and the Protestant communities. Very secret talks began between the different groups. They went on for many years. People called **mediators** were a great help. Mediators are people who are not directly involved in the struggle. They can talk to both sides, sometimes together and sometimes separately. In 1998 a peace agreement was signed. It is called the Good Friday Agreement because it was signed just before Easter that year. Terrorists on both sides promised to give up their weapons and to stop their violence.

mediator: someone who is in the middle, who helps other people to find an agreement

In Northern Ireland anger and hate have not disappeared altogether. A very few people still carry on with terrorism. But almost all the population wants to live in peace.

See the Londonderry/ Derry Peace Bridge in Q38. When will terrorism end? (p 93)

A mediator can help to solve problems and make peace

Talking about Terrorism: Responding to Children's Questions 71

Main answers which are better suited to Upper KS2 in green type

Tips for teachers along with explanations and guidance for sensitive handling of issues where appropriate

Key vocabulary with definitions highlighted in each question (full glossary available at the back of the book)

Handy cross-referencing to related topics and key themes in other questions answered in the book

Relevant photographs and illustrations that help to bring the whole topic or an incident to life

Other special features used

True story
Positive stories of action, recovery and reconciliation

True story

Super hound Brewster – No ordinary dog!

www.watfordobserver.co.uk/news/14212310.Police_dog_Brewster_now_set_to_lap_up_the_good_life/

Brewster is an English Springer-Spaniel. He was born in North Yorkshire but he had so much energy that his owners couldn't look after him properly, so they gave him to the police. Brewster worked for 10 years in a special police dog team with his trainer PC Dave Pert. Brewster's incredible nose led the police to discover large amounts of drugs and weapons. Brewster also helped the police to find and arrest the criminals who were trying to hide them. Brewster retired from the police force at the age of 13. PC Pert said he would be spending his retirement at home, enjoying all his favourite hobbies like chasing tennis balls, swimming in rivers, eating dog treats and napping.

Information box
Historical accounts of significant people and groups

Lower KS2 Upper KS2 **Information box**

The Suffragettes

Nowadays most people think of the Suffragettes as a group of very brave women. About a hundred years ago they were called terrorists. At that time women could not vote in a general election in Britain or be members of parliament. Many women (and some men too) were very angry about this. They formed a group to protest about it. They were called Suffragettes because they wanted women's **suffrage** – the right to vote. The Suffragettes wanted to send a message to members of parliament that they were angry and wanted things to change.

Teacher's tip
Simplify as appropriate for LKS2.

suffrage: the right to vote

Example
Brief descriptions of actual terrorist events

EXAMPLE

In June 2015 a white man entered a Methodist church in Charleston, South Carolina, and shot dead nine black Americans who were members of a prayer group. Some people call this terrorism; others call it 'hate crime'.

Storyline
A simple short story about the human tragedy of conflict is told through the loss of a beloved teddy bear, whose return to his rightful owner becomes a symbol of hope and peace.

Questions 39 and 40 are supplementary 'If' questions of a more specific nature covering likely emotive and emotional enquiries. These may not be appropriate to your class, but the answers are there to be used should you feel you need them.

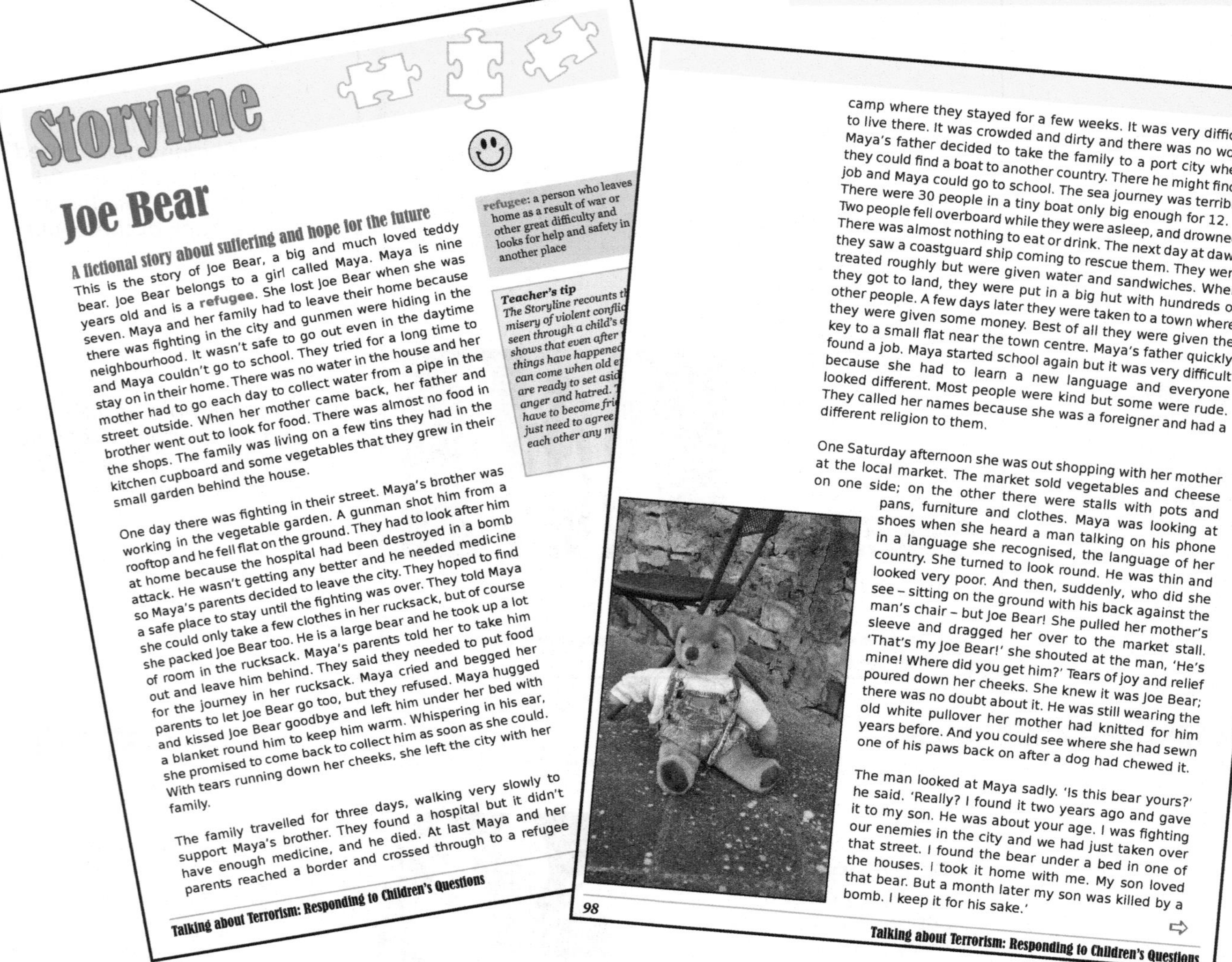

Storyline

Joe Bear

A fictional story about suffering and hope for the future

This is the story of Joe Bear, a big and much loved teddy bear. Joe Bear belongs to a girl called Maya. Maya is nine years old and is a **refugee**. She lost Joe Bear when she was seven. Maya and her family had to leave their home because there was fighting in the city and gunmen were hiding in the neighbourhood. It wasn't safe to go out even in the daytime and Maya couldn't go to school. They tried for a long time to stay on in their home. There was no water in the house and her mother had to go each day to collect water from a pipe in the street outside. When her mother came back, her father and brother went out to look for food. There was almost no food in the shops. The family was living on a few tins they had in the kitchen cupboard and some vegetables that they grew in their small garden behind the house.

One day there was fighting in their street. Maya's brother was working in the vegetable garden. A gunman shot him from a rooftop and he fell flat on the ground. They had to look after him at home because the hospital had been destroyed in a bomb attack. He wasn't getting any better and he needed medicine so Maya's parents decided to leave the city. They hoped to find a safe place to stay until the fighting was over. They told Maya she could only take a few clothes in her rucksack, but of course she packed Joe Bear too. He is a large bear and he took up a lot of room in the rucksack. Maya's parents told her to take him out and leave him behind. They said they needed to put food for the journey in her rucksack. Maya cried and begged her parents to let Joe Bear go too, but they refused. Maya hugged and kissed Joe Bear goodbye and left him under her bed with a blanket round him to keep him warm. Whispering in his ear, she promised to come back to collect him as soon as she could. With tears running down her cheeks, she left the city with her family.

The family travelled for three days, walking very slowly to support Maya's brother. They found a hospital but it didn't have enough medicine, and he died. At last Maya and her parents reached a border and crossed through to a refugee

refugee: a person who leaves home as a result of war or other great difficulty and looks for help and safety in another place

Teacher's tip
The Storyline recounts th
misery of violent conflic
seen through a child's e
shows that even after
things have happened
can come when old e
are ready to set asid
anger and hatred.
have to become fri
just need to agree
each other any m

Talking about Terrorism: Responding to Children's Questions

camp where they stayed for a few weeks. It was very difficult to live there. It was crowded and dirty and there was no work. Maya's father decided to take the family to a port city where they could find a boat to another country. There he might find a job and Maya could go to school. The sea journey was terrible. There were 30 people in a tiny boat only big enough for 12. Two people fell overboard while they were asleep, and drowned. There was almost nothing to eat or drink. The next day at dawn they saw a coastguard ship coming to rescue them. They were treated roughly but were given water and sandwiches. When they got to land, they were put in a big hut with hundreds of other people. A few days later they were taken to a town where they were given some money. Best of all they were given the key to a small flat near the town centre. Maya's father quickly found a job. Maya started school again but it was very difficult because she had to learn a new language and everyone looked different. Most people were kind but some were rude. They called her names because she was a foreigner and had a different religion to them.

One Saturday afternoon she was out shopping with her mother at the local market. The market sold vegetables and cheese on one side; on the other there were stalls with pots and pans, furniture and clothes. Maya was looking at shoes when she heard a man talking on his phone in a language she recognised, the language of her country. She turned to look round. He was thin and looked very poor. And then, suddenly, who did she see – sitting on the ground with his back against the man's chair – but Joe Bear! She pulled her mother's sleeve and dragged her over to the market stall. 'That's my Joe Bear!' she shouted at the man, 'He's mine! Where did you get him?' Tears of joy and relief poured down her cheeks. She knew it was Joe Bear; there was no doubt about it. He was still wearing the old white pullover her mother had knitted for him years before. And you could see where she had sewn one of his paws back on after a dog had chewed it.

The man looked at Maya sadly. 'Is this bear yours?' he said. 'Really? I found it two years ago and gave it to my son. He was about your age. I was fighting our enemies in the city and we had just taken over that street. I found the bear under a bed in one of the houses. I took it home with me. My son loved that bear. But a month later my son was killed by a bomb. I keep it for his sake.'

98

Talking about Terrorism: Responding to Children's Questions

A full list of sources and ideas for further reading on *Prevent*, safeguarding and other topics concludes the book.

Footnote references

[1] http://srcd.org/sites/default/files/documents/spr29_2.pdf

[2] https://www.gov.uk/government/uploads/system/uploads/attachment_data/file/97976/prevent-strategy-review.pdf

[3] https://www.gov.uk/government/publications/prevent-duty-guidance

[4] http://www.npcc.police.uk/documents/TAM/2012/201210TAMChannelGuidance.pdf

[5] https://www.theguardian.com/uk-news/2016/mar/20/almost-4000-people-were-referred-to-uk-deradicalisation-scheme-channel-last-year; also https://www.theguardian.com/uk-news/2016/jul/12/teachers-made-one-third-of-referrals-to-prevent-strategy-in-2015

Where to start

> ***Teacher's tip***
> *It can be hard to choose how and when to approach the subject of terrorism. You could begin with a discussion of an event in the news, or with a question raised in the classroom. Here is a simple way of getting started.*

Terrorism is a very difficult subject to talk about. We often hear the word used on TV, at home and at school. Although we hear about 'terrorism' almost every day, it's hard to say exactly what it is. We know it involves violence and people being hurt, but we don't really know where it comes from or why it happens. The idea of this book is to think about all the questions we have about terrorism and then to look for answers to them. We'll be exploring terrorism from different angles. We'll be finding out what terrorism is and what it isn't. We'll be discovering what terrorists do and why. And we'll explore how terrorism starts and how it ends.

Imagine terrorism as a jigsaw with many different pieces. There are various ways of doing a jigsaw. One is to take all the pieces out of the box and lay them out in front of us. Then we look for the corner pieces and the straight edges because they give us an outline for the whole picture. We can leave the pieces with blue sky till the end. We won't really understand what the jigsaw is about until we find the right pieces and fit them together. That's what we'll be trying to do with terrorism. First, we look for the jigsaw pieces that we need to get started. These are our most important questions about terrorism. Once we have the questions we can start to look for answers. That's much more difficult. We may not be able to find all the pieces to finish the picture. In fact we almost certainly won't. Nobody has all the answers. There are many things we don't understand about terrorism. And there is almost nothing that we can be certain about. For these reasons it's a very difficult subject, for adults as well as for children.

The questions and answers we give in this book are mostly about terrorism, but we'll be studying other ideas as well. We'll be looking at how we can solve everyday problems in a peaceful way, how children have rights that are protected by special laws all over the world and how children can make the world a more peaceful place. We will learn that even when something terrible happens like a terrorist attack, something good can come out of it. And we will discover how very special and courageous people have helped to end terrorism and bring peace.

There are many more questions to ask than the ones in this book. You children will almost certainly think of some. The authors of the book would like to hear from you, and they will answer your questions if they can.

The most important questions about terrorism usually begin with the words: What...? Why...? Who...? Where...? How...? and When...? These words give us the guidelines for *Talking about Terrorism*.

1. What is terrorism?

terrorism: violence used to frighten people; violence for a reward

The very word 'terror-ism' helps us to understand what it is. **Terrorism** is all about terror. Terrorism is violence that makes people afraid and upset. It's *violence used to frighten people*, to stop them living in a free and open way: the way we live in Britain. The word terrorism on its own doesn't give us much information; it only tells us that it's violence of a certain kind. We could probably say that it is violence done by terrorists – people who are angry and full of hate. But it doesn't tell us who the terrorists are or where they come from. It doesn't tell us who they hate, or why. It certainly doesn't tell us what colour their skin is or what religion they belong to, if they have a religion at all. We can say that terrorism is almost always carried out by people who have strong ideas and beliefs. But the word tells us nothing about what these ideas and beliefs are.

regiment: a large, organised formation of soldiers

Terrorism is *a kind of war.* It is not like a war between two armies, with soldiers wearing uniform. Soldiers who fight for their country wear their country's flag sewn on to their uniforms. Everyone can see what country and what **regiment** they belong to. Terrorists are often fighting *against* their own country and its government. *Terrorism is usually started by a weaker group against a much stronger one,* like a government. The members of a terrorist group come together because they believe in the same things, but they could be of different nationalities. They don't wear a uniform and they usually keep what they do a secret.

Ask the children to write down any questions they have about terrorism and to put their questions into a box. The questions should then be put on a central whiteboard. Explain that you will try to answer these questions in the course of the lessons.

Alternatively invite them to draw something showing what the word *'terrorism'* or *'terrorist'* means to them, thinking carefully about the colours they will use.

Invite children to write a letter to a terrorist. If they could ask a terrorist six questions, what would they be?

Ask each child to work with a partner, playing a game of word association with the word *'terrorism'*. One partner should keep a note in a jotter of all the words which come to mind. These can be used in later activities.

The terrorism 'cooking pot'

Think of terrorism as a large cooking pot. When we make a particular dish, like a stew or a curry, we need to have certain ingredients in the pot. Terrorism has a number of ingredients too. If certain ingredients aren't in the pot then what we're looking at probably isn't terrorism. Here are some of the ingredients that we find in the terrorism cooking pot:

- violence used to make people frightened
- strong feelings of anger and hatred
- strong feelings that 'things aren't fair'; that no one will put wrong things right and that 'no one is on my side'
- the wish to take revenge against an enemy who is blamed for the unfairness
- the feeling that violence is the *only* way to change things, that violence is necessary

Some of the ingredients of the terrorism cooking pot

Strong feelings of anger and hatred, and that 'things aren't fair' are part of what make terrorists do what they do. These feelings aren't enough, of course, because many other people have the same feelings and don't use violence.

Upper KS2

The strong feelings that 'things aren't fair' and that no one will put wrong things right are called **grievances**. Where there is terrorism, we will always find people with grievances.
Other ingredients of the terrorism cooking pot include:

grievances: feelings of anger that wrong things have not been put right
civilians: people who are not members of the armed forces
political power: the power to decide how a community is run
publicity: a high level of attention from the public

- violence used against 'ordinary people' or **civilians** (people who are not part of the armed forces)
- ideas about violence and about the future that are shared with other people
- the desire for **political power** – that means the right to change the way a country or a community lives and how it is run
- violence that has a message – the message is for the government or the people in charge (It says the terrorists are angry and may use violence again if they don't get what they want.)
- the wish for **publicity** – that as many people as possible should hear about the attacks
- violence used to win something – we call it a reward

We can say that grievances are the *reasons* that terrorists have for using violence. But it's important to realise that many, many people have grievances but don't become terrorists. This is one of the most difficult things to understand about terrorism. Out of all the people in the world who are angry and who have grievances, why do a few become terrorists but most don't? The answer is, we really do not know. We can't find the jigsaw piece that fits this space. Experts think that some people may not be able to control their feelings of anger and hatred as well as others. This might be why they are more likely to use violence than others.

See Q30. How does someone become a terrorist? (p 75)

Invite children to make a list with at least five things/ingredients which would be present if we were to call something 'terrorism'.

If appropriate, invite the children to think about a terrorist attack that they remember. Which of the above 'ingredients' were involved? What happened?

2. What do terrorists do?

Terrorists carry out violent attacks. Often, they deliberately kill or injure people. Terrorists also attack important buildings, places where people meet up, and forms of transport that many people use. The ways in which they carry out their attacks are their *methods*. Their methods include shooting at people with guns or planting bombs and setting them off in crowded places like markets or shopping centres.

Sometimes terrorists attack what we call **infrastructure**. This means they attack and damage the buildings or the networks that provide us with important services. These include electricity cables or pylons, phone and Internet services, and oil, gas or water supplies. We need all these services in our daily lives. We need them for our homes, in schools, in hospitals and in places where people work. They are necessary to make our cars, trains and buses run and to make our planes fly.

infrastructure: buildings, transport and other networks that provide important services

Victims and targets of terrorism

When terrorists carry out attacks, they are attacking two lots of people at the same time. The people they kill or injure are called the **victims** of terrorism. Often the victims are ordinary men, women and children who just happen to be in a certain place when the attack happens. Another name for 'ordinary people' is **civilians** – people who are not members of the armed forces. The terrorists also want to frighten another group of people. They are the people who are in charge of things, for example in parliament or government. We call these people the **target**.

victim: someone who is hurt or killed (for example in a terrorist attack)
civilians: people who are not members of the armed forces
target: the main goal or object (that is attacked)

They are important because they are the people who have power and who can change things. They can give the terrorists what they want, or not. Terrorists carry out an attack because they want to send a message to the people in charge. The message is: 'Just look at what we've done, we will do this again unless you do what we want.'

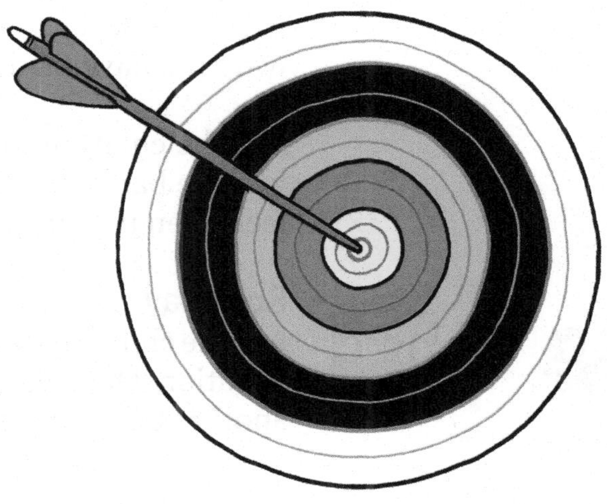

Terrorists attack both ordinary people (victims) and the people in charge (the target)

Show the children a picture with a coloured hoop in the centre and four smaller hoops on the outside. Explain that the central hoop is the terrorist target, the main enemy. The smaller hoops are the bystanders and the victims. Give the children a photocopy of PCM1 (p 103) or ask them to draw it. Ask them to label on the hoops the target and victims of terrorism using key words from the above text for example governments, parliaments, civilians, ordinary men, women and children.

hostage: someone who is held prisoner by a person or group of people

Terrorists don't always hurt people. Sometimes they *threaten* to hurt people. They take people prisoner and then threaten to kill them. When people are taken prisoner for this reason we call them **hostages**.

bargain: an agreement

Terrorists take hostages in order to make a **bargain**. They want a *reward* for letting the hostages go free. When you make a bargain, what happens? You give away something that another person wants in order to have something that you want. It's an exchange, or a swap. We all bargain with our friends and parents from a young age.

Tina is a seven-year-old girl and a keen football fan. When the World Cup was on TV, Tina loved to watch it. The problem was that the football matches were shown after her bedtime. A bargain was struck.

Ask the children to say why we make bargains. What kind of bargain will Tina have made?

Ask the children to recall a time when they made a bargain. Who was the bargain with, what was agreed or achieved? How did they feel when the bargain had been made?

Role-play

Ask the children to devise a role-play in pairs depicting a bargaining situation. Once they have the role-play, invite them to share it with another pair. Can the second pair work out what the bargain was?

Upper KS2

Information box

Kidnapping, hostage-taking and hijacking

Terrorist methods that involve trying to make a bargain include: **kidnapping**, hostage-taking and **hijacking**.

kidnap: to take and keep someone in a secret place against their wishes, usually to make a bargain
hijack: to take over a vehicle, keeping the passengers as hostages
ransom: a sum of money paid to free a hostage

Kidnapping means taking people away to a secret place and hiding them. No one knows where the hostages are except the people who are guarding them. *Hostage-taking* is different. If terrorists enter a building and take hostages, everyone knows where they are. They might be in a restaurant or in a building or in an aircraft. It's difficult to free them because the terrorists might kill them.

A *hijacking* is when terrorists take over a vehicle like a bus, a train or a plane. They point a gun at the driver or pilot and order him to take the vehicle to a particular place. They keep the passengers as hostages. Then the terrorists tell the government what bargain they want to make. If they don't get what they want, they say they will kill the hostages.

EXAMPLE

In Sydney Australia, on 15–16 December 2014, a gunman held 18 people hostage for 16 hours in a siege at a Lindt chocolate café. Two hostages were killed: one by the gunman and another accidentally by police. The gunman was also killed.

Police must take great care when they try to free hostages

What sort of things do terrorists bargain for when they have hostages?

The terrorists might ask for:

- an exchange of prisoners (This means they will free the hostages if the government allows some of their friends in prison to go free.)
- a lot of money (The money paid to free a hostage is called a **ransom**. Terrorists need money, both to pay for food and places to live and also to buy weapons and explosives.)
- a plane to fly to another country where they will be safe from arrest
- a bargain with the government: for example the terrorists may say, 'We'll kill the hostages unless you bring back your country's soldiers from … (another country)'

3. What do terrorists want?

Terrorists always have things that they want. That's why they carry out terrorist attacks. They want to win a *reward* from using violence. The reward is what we call their *goal*. Their goal is not just for one person or a small group but for a bigger community.

The goals of terrorism

Here are some of the things that terrorists want:

- ❖ *freedom from someone or from something* (They want freedom to live under their own rules.)
- ❖ *to change people's behaviour* (They want to frighten the people who are in charge, who are running things, into changing the way a country or an area is run. They also want to change the behaviour of ordinary people. They want to make ordinary people afraid to go to the market, to travel or to enjoy relaxing in the way they choose.)
- ❖ *to send a message* (The message is that they are angry and they will carry out more attacks unless things change.)
- ❖ *to punish an enemy* (They are angry about what is happening in a particular country or area. They think unfair things are being done to people they care about. They blame an enemy for this and they want to take revenge.)
- ❖ *to divide people, to make people angry and hate each other* (They want us to believe that people of different races or faiths cannot live together peacefully. They don't want us to stand together and support each other.)
- ❖ *everyone to pay attention* (Another way of saying this is that they want **publicity** – they want everyone to talk about them and their attacks. For terrorists, the more people who see and hear about their attacks the better it is.)

publicity: a high level of attention from the public

Lower KS2

Teacher's tip
Encourage discussion of: being loud in the playground; being outstanding at sport or another activity; being cheeky; having elaborate hair or clothes. What does this attention achieve?

Ask the children if they have ever voted for a class representative for a school council. *What happens?* The children who want to represent the class sometimes run a campaign, put up posters around school and persuade others to vote for them. They want attention as they hope to be elected. This is a positive way of gaining attention.

In pairs, invite the children to discuss other ways that children sometimes gain attention in school.

Ask children to think of examples of changing behaviour, for example: As they walk to school each day they meet a group of children who are unkind and say nasty things about them and their friends. What choices would they have in this situation? One choice would be to change their route to school to avoid the particular group of children. If they do that, they have changed their behaviour. What would a different choice be? Ask children to use this example, or one of their own, to represent the before and after behaviour.

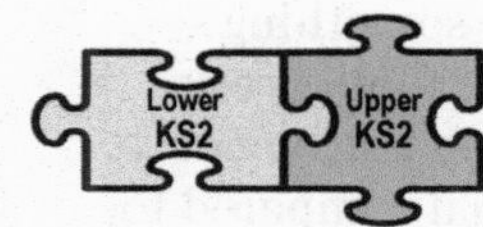

Terrorists also want the government to pass laws that make us less free. They want the government to **react** to their violence, for example by bringing in new laws that are very strict.

react: to respond, act as a direct result of something

An example of this might be a population that is frightened after a series of terrorist attacks. Most of these attacks have taken place at night. The government brings in a new law which says no one can go out after 9 o'clock at night. Then the terrorists could say – 'You think your country is free and open. Now see what we made you do!' In other words, terrorists want to make us less free because of what they make us do. If the government takes away our freedom by making strict new laws then the terrorists have won.

4. What do the terrorists' families think about it?

It can happen that some members of the family agree with using violence. There have been examples of this, when two brothers have taken part in the same attack. They knew they could trust one another, and they shared the same feelings of anger and hatred. This doesn't seem to happen much with parents and children. Usually parents know nothing at all about a son or daughter's decision to join a terrorist group. Then when it happens they are horrified. Sometimes family members or friends may be worried. There could be warning signs. Maybe a son or daughter starts to behave in a strange way. Perhaps he or she starts to say that terrorism is a good thing, that violence is the only way to solve a problem. Or they start to say especially hateful things about another community or group of people. Even then it doesn't mean someone is going

extremist: something or someone that is very different, very strong or very unusual compared to others

See Q31. How can we stop someone becoming a terrorist? (p 79)

to be a terrorist. The son or daughter may have very strong or **extremist** opinions. They may not be planning to do anything at all. It may be that they are going through a particularly bad time for other reasons, which they will get over after a while. But if family members are worried then they may have to ask for help.

Circle time activity

Invite children to say how they would respond to someone saying hateful things.

Invite children to discuss how they would respond to someone saying hateful things.

5. What are the consequences of terrorism?

The consequences of terrorism are suffering and sadness. Violence causes more violence, and it's very hard to stop it once it starts. Terrorism almost never brings happiness or anything good. Terrorism doesn't build anything, it destroys things. People are injured and killed on both sides of a terrorist fight. Even on the side that wins a victory there will still be sadness. Children will have lost parents, brothers and sisters, parents will have lost sons or daughters. The effects of terrorism last a very long time. Even when peace comes it may take years for anger and hate to disappear. Suffering is like a deep cut on a leg. It may be less painful for a while and the wound seems to heal over, but it doesn't take much to open it up again. Because terrorism is a kind of war, it has similar effects to war. It destroys towns and villages, homes and schools. It destroys water and food supplies. Families may have to escape to another town or country. The countries that have suffered most from terrorism are Syria, Iraq, Afghanistan and Nigeria. That's why we see so many **refugees** from those countries. European countries are mostly very peaceful and citizens have the right to vote in elections. This means we can change things in a peaceful way.

refugee: a person who leaves home as a result of war or other great difficulty and looks for help and safety in another place

6. What do TV, Internet and social media have to do with terrorism?

TV, Internet and social media are all very important for terrorists. When terrorists carry out an attack, especially if the attack is in a big city, it will be shown on TV news a few minutes later. People will rush over and film the scene on their mobile phones and share it with their friends. The terrorists may film their own attacks and post the videos on social media. Terrorists want as many people as possible to see what they do and to pay attention to them. They want to send a message to governments and important people. Terrorists want their message to go across the world. TV and video help this to happen.

Imagine going into a cave and shouting out your name. What happens? There is an echo and you hear your name repeated over and over again, loudly. Or if you skim a pebble across a very calm pond it sends ripples for a long distance. This is what terrorists want. They want to send their message around the world. The message is that they are angry. They want to tell the people in charge of things to change their behaviour. If the people in charge don't change their behaviour, the terrorists threaten to carry out another attack.

Journalists have a duty to report the stories that happen around the world, so of course they must show and tell us what has happened. But sometimes they only show the horror. They don't say enough about the courage of the rescuers, for example.

See Q35. How can anything good ever come out of terrorism? (p 85)

Terrorists want the world to be watching and listening. They want everyone to pay attention. The whole world becomes the **audience** for what they have done. In this way we can say that terrorism is like a performance. It's a performance that can be seen all round the world. Some people say that the **media** (TV, radio, newspapers and Internet) give too much attention to terrorism.

audience: people who listen to and watch a performance
media: TV, radio, newspapers and Internet

Some terrorist organisations use the Internet and social media to ask people to join them. They set up websites that send messages of hate and anger. They try to stir up hate in the

people who visit the websites. They want to make people angry so that they take revenge against an 'enemy'. The enemy could be in Britain or abroad. Some of the violent messages are for young men. They show videos and give lessons about fighting and making bombs. There are messages that encourage young men and even boys to leave Britain and become 'foreign fighters'. Sometimes the messages are for girls. They ask girls to leave their homes and go abroad too. They want girls to be brides for the fighting men. They say that girls have a very important job to do. In fact the girls who do leave home and go abroad to marry fighters often have a terrible time. The men treat them very badly and they are hardly ever allowed to leave their homes. They have to do exactly what the men say.

Debate

Split the class into two groups and hold a debate on whether TV and the media should report terrorist stories or not. If so, how should they do this?

7. What can children do to make the world more peaceful?

There are lots of ways that children as well as adults can make the world more peaceful. Here are some of them:

- be thoughtful and kind to other people
- show respect for people who are different to ourselves
- look for peaceful ways of solving problems
- stand together when bad things happen

Invite the class to think of others.

Be thoughtful and kind to other people

Being thoughtful and kind to other people are things we can do every day. Children can help younger children, or children who are not as strong as themselves. When you go for a walk in a park or in the countryside you can respect the environment by not dropping litter. Caring for other people and caring about the environment are two things that go together and can be part of daily school life. Both of them involve thinking about

Children can all help to make the world more peaceful

the world outside ourselves. If you learn more about the wider world, you realise how difficult life can be for people who have to live in places where violent things happen every day. More than a million people arrived in Europe in 2015 to escape from conflict. A quarter of them were children. Learning about other people's lives is very important, because it makes us realise how lucky we are in Britain.

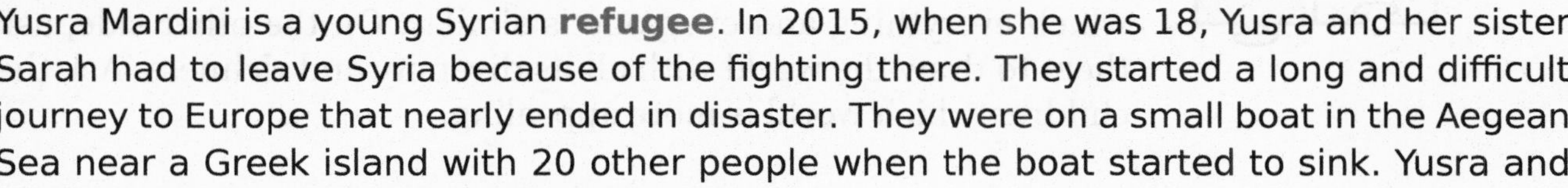

Olympic swimmer Yusra Mardini

Yusra Mardini is a young Syrian **refugee**. In 2015, when she was 18, Yusra and her sister Sarah had to leave Syria because of the fighting there. They started a long and difficult journey to Europe that nearly ended in disaster. They were on a small boat in the Aegean Sea near a Greek island with 20 other people when the boat started to sink. Yusra and Sarah were the only ones who could swim. They jumped into the water and managed to push and pull the boat to shore. A year later Yusra became one of 10 athletes in the Refugee Olympic Team at the Olympic Games in Rio de Janeiro, Brazil. She won her swimming heat in the 100m butterfly race. Afterwards she said, 'I want to make all the refugees proud of me. It would show that even if we had a tough journey, we can achieve something.'

Yusra Mardini after winning her swimming heat

refugee: a person who leaves home as a result of war or other great difficulty and looks for help and safety in another place

Show respect for people who are different to ourselves

Showing respect for other people and for the differences between us is an important way of making the world more peaceful. Even in Britain there are many differences between people and how they live. British people dress in many different ways, they have different faiths and they have different ideas about how to live. Even if we don't understand all the differences we can still be respectful and tolerant of other people. Another big difference is in how people speak. Every area of Britain has its own accent and some parts even have their own language, like Welsh or Gaelic. A lot of people speak English at school but other languages at home, like Urdu or Polish. These differences are good and are part of what makes life interesting. Think of how boring it would be if we had to listen to the same piece of music or wear the same colour of clothes every single day. Imagine if every flower were the same colour, or we could only ever eat one colour of food. After a thunderstorm we enjoy looking at a rainbow. The best thing about a rainbow is that all the colours are there together. Differences or **diversity** is something we should celebrate. One of the great things about Britain is that people are different.

diversity: differences, variety

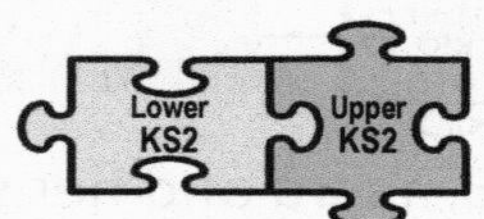

Invite children to divide a page into two halves. On one side, ask them to draw an image of a world without diversity, a world in which everything and everyone is similar. On the other side, ask them to draw the world with all its diversity and richness. Ask the children which world is more appealing.

Look for peaceful ways of solving problems

Looking for peaceful ways of solving problems is another very important thing that children can do. This means not becoming angry if you don't agree with someone. It means trying to see the other person's point of view. Of course there are times when we all lose our temper and get cross. But if we take a deep breath and count to five, we can probably think of a peaceful way to solve a problem. If something bad has been done to you, you won't make things better by doing something bad back. In fact taking revenge is likely to make things worse not better. Most things can be solved by talking them through. If the problem is serious and very difficult to solve, having another person there as a 'referee' can be helpful.

Stand together when bad things happen

If something bad happens to a family or a community, it's very important for everyone to stand together. Sometimes terrorists want to make us hate people of a particular religion or community. If they divide us and make us hate each other, then they have won a victory. It's important not to let that happen.

When people stand together to remember victims of a terrorist attack or some other tragedy, we call it a **vigil**. A vigil is usually held in a public place, often in the evening. Sometimes it is in the exact place where an attack happened. People light candles and lay flowers. They stand quietly, thinking their thoughts and being sad. The candles glow in the darkness. This is a sign that those who have died are still alive in the memories of the people who are there. At the same time the people who have gathered together are sending a message to the terrorists. The message is, 'we are not afraid, our lives will carry on. You will not make us hate.'

EXAMPLE

People in countries all over the world stood together to comfort France after the terrorist attacks there in 2015. On 13 November, 130 people were killed in a series of shootings and suicide bombings in a concert hall, a football stadium and at several cafés and restaurants. The attacks were claimed by Islamic State.

Children in schools in Britain sang the French **national anthem**. Even rival English football teams sang the French national anthem before their matches. Capital cities in many countries lit up their most important buildings in blue, white and red – the colours of the French flag. All these things were very comforting to the French people at a time of great sadness.

national anthem: a song to celebrate a country

See Q21. Who are Al-Qaeda and Islamic State? (p 60)

vigil: a watch, a silent standing together of people to remember an event

Sydney Opera House was lit up with the colours of the French flag to stand together with France after the attacks, even though the cities are more than 10,000 miles apart

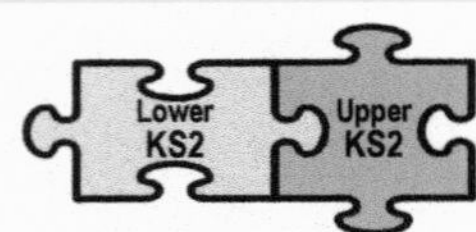

Pete Seeger
www.youtube.com/watch?v=QhnPVP23rzo
Joan Baez
www.youtube.com/watch?v=RkNsEH1GD7Q
Brandon Le – Bataclan
www.youtube.com/watch?v=Hft06pyiMac

Explain that not being afraid and standing together are part of a famous song called 'We shall overcome'. Show a video clip of Pete Seeger or Joan Baez and explain how the song was sung at civil rights rallies in the USA. Discuss the song and what it means with the children.

Five-year-old Brandon Le was standing with his father outside the Bataclan theatre in Paris on the day after the terrorist attacks there when he was interviewed on TV. (Show YouTube clip with English subtitles.) Many people, including children, had brought flowers and candles to remember the people who had died. Brandon told the TV journalist that his family would have to move house because bad people could shoot them with guns. His father said, 'No, there can be bad people anywhere but Paris is our home. We're OK, they might have guns but we have flowers. Everyone is putting flowers down; it's to fight against the guns. The flowers and candles are here to protect us.' Turning guns into flowers would make the world more peaceful, as this cheerful poem, reproduced on PCM2 (p 104), shows:

If mice could roar

If mice could roar
And elephants soar
And trees grow up in the sky
If tigers could dine
On biscuits and wine,
And the fattest of men could fly!
If pebbles could sing
And bells never ring
And teachers were lost in the post;
If a tortoise could run
And losses be won,
And bullies be buttered on toast;
If a song brought a shower
And a gun grew a flower
This world would be nicer than most!

Ruskin Bond : Ruskin Bond's Book of Verse, Penguin Books India (2007)

Lower KS2 Upper KS2

True story

Jo Cox

Here is one family that has shown love rather than hate at a time of tragedy: Jo Cox was a British member of parliament who was murdered near her home in Yorkshire in June 2016. The man who killed her was angry because she often said in her speeches that Britain should give more help to refugees, especially from Syria. She had a husband and two young children. Jo's husband said that it was very cruel for her family to lose her, but that they were unbelievably lucky to have had her in their lives for so long. He said Jo wouldn't want her killing to lead to more hatred. She would have wanted her death to be a way of bringing peace and love.

See Q35. How can anything good ever come out of terrorism? (p 85)

Jo Cox, a British member of parliament, who supported help for refugees

Ask the children to think back to the ingredients which went into the terrorism cooking pot (see p 25). Invite them to come up with a list of ingredients for a cooking pot of peace.

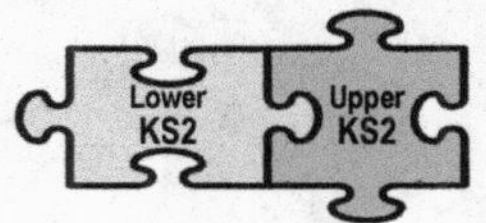

Invite the children to write a poem with the title, 'Children of the world'.

8. Why is terrorism different from other violence?

Violence that is not terrorism

It may seem strange, but we can learn about what terrorism IS by knowing what is NOT terrorism. There are many different kinds of violence in the world that are not terrorism. Terrorism is *man-made*. It's a kind of violence that belongs only to human beings. We don't find terrorism in nature and we don't find it in the animal world.

Nature is often violent. Think of earthquakes, tsunamis, volcano eruptions and flooding. None of these is terrorism. Wild animals use violence. When we watch nature programmes on TV, we see lions and tigers hunting other animals. That isn't terrorism either. Why not? Because lions and tigers have to kill in order to feed themselves and their families. When they're hungry, they hide behind bushes or in long grass until an antelope or other prey comes along, then the big cats jump out. Lions and tigers kill because they need to survive. Their violence is an *instinct*, it's not a choice. They don't sit around making plans to go out and kill antelopes next Thursday morning. Animals may **terrorise** other animals but we can't call them terrorists.

to terrorise: to make something or someone very frightened

Human beings don't have to kill other people in order to survive. When human beings use violence, it's a choice. They want a *reward*. Think of an example we all know about: bullying.

Events in nature are often violent and can cause terror, but we do not call them terrorism

Bullying sometimes involves violence, and people who bully want a reward. The reward might be a penknife or a mobile phone or money. Or the reward might just be to have power over someone else for a while. Bullying is not terrorism. Like someone who bullies, a terrorist wants to *have power over other people*. But the power the terrorist wants is not just for him, he wants it for other people too.

Think of another example of someone who wants power over other people: a bank robber. The bank robber runs into the bank, points a gun at everyone and says 'Hands up or I'll shoot!' He may not actually use violence but he *threatens* to use it. He says he'll shoot anyone who doesn't do as he says. He wants to terrorise people. He wants to make them frightened so they will obey him. He makes everyone stand with their hands up except the bank manager. She is in charge of the money. She passes banknotes across the counter while he puts them into a suitcase. Then he runs outside with the suitcase, jumps into a car and drives away.

Bank robbers are criminals but they aren't terrorists, as a rule. What's the difference? Terrorists and bank robbers commit crimes, sometimes violent crimes, but the difference is in *why* they do it. The bank robber wants a reward, but the reward is just for him. He wants to spend the money on himself, perhaps on a new car or expensive clothes or to go abroad. Terrorists want a reward for themselves and other people – they see themselves as champions or heroes. They are fighting for rewards that – they think – will help other people. The bank robber terrorises the people in the bank, but he doesn't hate them, he's not angry with them. He doesn't want to take revenge on them for anything. Terrorists have strong feelings like anger and hatred, they believe that wrong or very unfair things have been done and not put right. They want to take revenge for the unfairness.

True and false cards

Give the children 12 cards on PCM3 (p 105) that make statements about terrorism. Some of the statements are true, some are false. Ask the children in small groups to sort them accordingly. Feel free to modify or add your own as appropriate.

Scissors

Earthquakes and tsunamis are a type of terrorism.	If a person feels terrorised, the reason must be terrorism.	Terrorism just happens, it isn't organised or planned.	Terrorists only want money as a reward.
People are always responsible for acts of terrorism.	Terrorists usually want a reward just for themselves.	Terrorists believe that talking is as good as violence.	Terrorists often feel that something in the world is unfair.
Bullying is a type of terrorism.	Terrorists are often interested in politics.	It would be fair to call a bank robber a terrorist.	Terrorism also exists in the animal world.

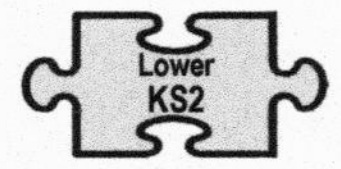

Draw a poster showing clearly what terrorism is or isn't, using examples given.

political power: the power to decide how a community is run
democracy: a country where all adults have a say in how things are run, for example by electing members of parliament

Like the bank robber, the terrorist uses or threatens violence, and the terrorist wants a reward. But unlike the bank robber, terrorists use violence because they want to change how things are done. They want **political power.** That means the power to decide the way a country or an area is run. There's nothing wrong with wanting political power. In a **democracy** like Britain, everyone over 18 has political power: the right to vote. They can vote for their local council, and they can elect members of parliament (MPs) every five years. If people don't like what the MPs are doing they can vote for someone else next time, or they can protest about it. Peaceful protest is allowed. It's a freedom that we have in Britain, a precious one. Terrorism is the opposite of democracy. It's a kind of war. Terrorists want to frighten people into giving them power. They want to change how things are done by violence. They don't believe in democracy.

Invite children to design a PowerPoint presentation showing how terrorism is different from other forms of violence.

9. Why are terrorists so angry and full of hate?

Terrorists are angry because they feel very strongly that things are not fair. They believe that they or their community have been treated badly. Terrorists need to blame someone for this and the person or people who are blamed are 'the enemy'. They feel hate for 'the enemy', which is usually a government or a ruling group.

Hatred – a strong dislike of something or someone – is one of the strongest feelings that human beings have, and it can go very deep. Sometimes hatred is so strong that people feel it is just as much a part of them as an arm or a leg is. Hatred may come from something that happened a long time ago, like quarrels or wars. In this case it is passed down from generation to generation. It can be kept going by stories told between friends, families or people who were on the same side in the quarrel or war.

Think about a tall tree with deep roots. The roots spread far under the ground. The longer the tree lives the deeper and stronger the roots are. Hate can be like this too: the longer it goes on the deeper it becomes.

Hatred is like a tree with deep roots, the longer it goes on the deeper it becomes

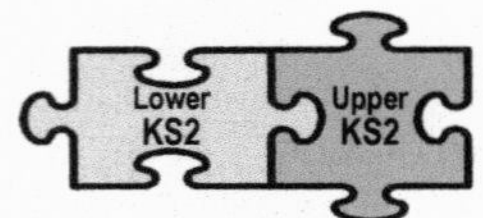

Love and hate activities

Invite children to think briefly of things they hate, encouraging superficial 'hates' for example types of food or music, wasps, spiders.

Heart template

Ask them what the opposite of hate is. Give the children a template of a heart and discuss what it represents. On the heart, ask the children to write down people or things which they love.

Ask the children to stand up in pairs. In each pair one child is A, the other is B. Ask Child A to think of someone or people whom they love, and to use the force of love to push up their arms. Child B tries to hold their arms down. Now ask Child A to think of something they hate in the world and their arms should collapse. The outcome should be that love is so much stronger than hate. Ask the class to sketch this activity as a poster to demonstrate the difference between love and hate.

Nelson Mandela, the first black president of South Africa, said this:

> *No one is born hating another person because of the colour of his skin, or his background, or his religion. People must learn to hate, and if they can learn to hate, they can be taught to love, for love comes more naturally to the human heart than its opposite.*

See Q27. Where can we see that peace has won over terrorism? (p 68) and Q38. When will terrorism end? (p 92)

Invite the class to discuss this statement.

humiliated: made to feel worthless, unimportant

Hate is not always an old feeling; it can be quite new and still be very strong. Terrorists may feel hate because they or their families have been treated badly. They may feel **humiliated.** Being humiliated means being treated without respect, as if they are 'second-class citizens'. They imagine that people in other communities are doing fine, but they themselves have no hopes and no future. They hate the people that they blame for this situation. They want to take revenge for the unfairness they feel. Sometimes they hate their own lives and they need someone to blame for that.

Some kinds of terrorism have their roots in hate for another race or for another religion. This kind of terrorism also comes from fear: fear that the other religious or racial group will become too powerful. Terrorists often feel that they have to use violence to protect their community from attack.

There have been many terrorist attacks against African-Americans in the United States. One of the worst periods was in the 1960s, when Dr Martin Luther King Jr was leading the struggle for **civil rights**. Many attacks were carried out by groups of white Americans who hated African-Americans. They believed that African-Americans shouldn't have the same rights as they had. They thought that white people were better and that black Americans were 'second-class citizens'. They were afraid that they would win equal rights with whites. Even today attacks against African-Americans continue.

civil rights: rights that all citizens of a country enjoy

EXAMPLE

In June 2015 a white man entered a Methodist church in Charleston, South Carolina, and shot dead nine black Americans who were members of a prayer group. Some people call this terrorism; others call it 'hate crime'.

Terrorist attacks have been carried out against Jewish people in schools, museums and synagogues by people who hate Jews and are afraid of them. These are ideas that belonged to Adolf Hitler and the Nazi party in Germany in the 1930s. They led to what we call the Holocaust and the murder of around six million Jews in concentration camps during World War 2.

Many mosques have been attacked by people who hate Muslims. They don't want to see Islam becoming more important in the country where they live. The people who carry out these attacks blame all Muslims for terrorist attacks carried out by a very few. Nearly all Muslims disagree with these attacks so it is quite wrong to blame them. Most Muslims want to live in peace with people of other faiths and beliefs.

See Q33. How can we change things we don't like? (p 81) and Q18. Who is a terrorist? (p 54)

10. Why do people say that terrorism is about religion?

Some of the terrorism we see today is violence used for religious reasons. Terrorists often say that they are following the commands of a religious leader or a religious book. They are ready to kill other people or to die because they think their god will be very pleased with them. They think they will go to heaven or paradise more quickly. They say they are helping that religion. In fact they are harming it. Terrorist leaders often trick people and they twist what the religious teaching says. They pretend that killing other people is what their religion asks them to do, but in fact it is not. If terrorists believe what they are doing is right, they don't feel sorry for their victims. They don't think that the lives of their victims matter.

People often say that religion and terrorism are connected. In fact the main religions all have messages of peace and love.

Show pupils pictures of different religious symbols and key words which are common to all faiths and some which are specific. Include buildings and places of worship. Ask the class what aspects most religions share.

Encourage them to come up with answers such as:

- they have someone or something that is worshipped
- they have rules of behaviour
- they call for kindness to one's neighbour, help for the poor
- they call for respect and compassion for other people
- they call for respect for parents
- they have goals of peace and justice
- they have buildings for worship (for example, church, mosque, synagogue, gurdwara)

We say that some kinds of terrorism are done 'in the name of' a religion to show that there is a difference between what the religion says and what the terrorists are doing. Terrorism has been used 'in the name of' all the major religions – Christianity, Judaism, Hinduism, Islam, Sikhism and even Buddhism, which has non-violence as one of its most important rules. Often the terrorist leaders twist what the religious teaching says. They do this to persuade people to follow them. They make up stories that are not true. They use religion as a way to **justify** their violence. To justify means they find reasons to say something is the right thing to do. They use religion like a cloak. The cloak covers up the truth – that what they are doing is terrorism.

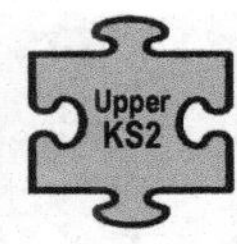

justify: to find or show reasons for doing something

11. Why do people put flowers down and light candles after a terrorist attack?

Signs of remembrance

People put candles and flowers down to remember the people who have been injured or killed – the victims of terrorism. The place where they put the flowers and candles may be the place where the attack happened or it may be a nearby square or garden. People find it comforting to come together and share their sadness. Doing this also shows the terrorists that they are not afraid. People write messages for the person who has died. If children have died, people sometimes leave a toy or a teddy bear. Candles remind us that even when people die their light still glows and we will remember them. Flowers are cheerful and colourful. Roses in particular make us think of love, happiness and peace. After the Paris attacks, a little boy told his father that the family would have to move house because of the bad men with guns. His father said, 'No, they have guns but we have flowers. The candles and flowers are there to protect us.' What he meant was that being peaceful was the best way to fight violence. He meant that people should fight hate with love. Dr Martin Luther King Jr also said that people should fight hate with love. He said:

See Q7. What can children do to make the world more peaceful? (p 34)

See Q33. How can we change things we don't like? (p 81)

> *Darkness cannot drive out darkness; only light can do that. Hate cannot drive out hate, only love can do that.*

People light candles and put flowers down to remember the victims of terrorism

Ask the children to fold an A4 sheet of paper in half. On one side ask the children to draw or write anything that they associate with light. On the other side anything they associate with dark. Which side is more appealing and positive?

Story of Pandora's box

Large packing box

Word cards

Show the children a large packing box. Inside it, place cards to represent the evils and hurts in the world. Read the story of Pandora's box. Dramatise the story by pulling out the terrible things one by one. Pause as you come towards the end as there is one thing left in the box. It is HOPE. It is hope that people hold on to and unite around. Ask the children to write a modern adaptation of Pandora's box. Would they put different things in the box? What would be left at the bottom?

12. Why do terrorists kill innocent people that they don't know?

Teacher's tip
The remaining questions in this section may be more appropriate for Upper Key Stage 2.

There are three main reasons for this. The first reason is that they don't really think about the people they hurt as human beings. They don't think about them having friends and parents or children and families. They see them as **symbols**: they represent a country or a government that the terrorists hate. In their minds they take out the human part of their victims, they are 'things' and they don't have feelings. This makes it easier for terrorists to use violence. Their victims are symbols or ideas rather than real people.

symbol: an example or picture that represents, or is a sign of, something else

The second reason is that terrorists don't think that their victims are innocent. They think their victims are 'the enemy', and deserve to be killed or injured. Terrorists want to punish people for living in a certain way. They want to punish their behaviour.

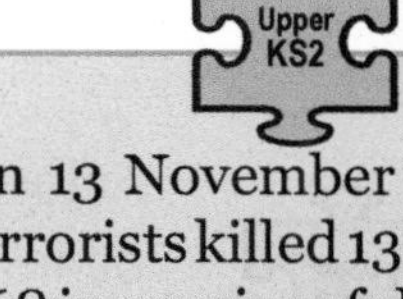

EXAMPLE

On 13 November 2015, Islamic State terrorists killed 130 people and injured 368 in a series of shootings and suicide bombings in Paris. They attacked a concert hall, a football stadium and several cafes and restaurants. These were all places where people went to have fun and relax together, to eat and drink. Islamic State wanted to terrorise the French people and they wanted to make them afraid to go out.

The third reason is that terrorists want to take revenge on people who have voted for a government that they (the terrorists) hate. In the case of the Paris attacks, the government had sent the French air force to bomb an area of Syria that was under the control of Islamic State. They wanted to punish the French people who had voted for that government. They also hoped the attack would force the French government to stop the bombing. They wanted to change the government's behaviour.

See Q21. Who are Al-Qaeda and Islamic State? (p 60)

13. Why do terrorists kill themselves as well as other people?

When terrorists kill themselves as well as other people, it's a deliberate choice. They know it will be more frightening. If they don't care about being hurt or about running away, they can kill more people. Attacks using suicide bombers, as they are called, kill four times as many people as other terrorist

sacrifice: a gift or offering of great value, usually as part of religious worship
martyr: a term used to describe someone who is put to death or dies because of their beliefs

attacks. Suicide bombers want to show that they are making a great **sacrifice**: a very valuable gift or offering. They want to show that their beliefs are so important that they are prepared to die for them. If they are fighting for religious beliefs, they think that they will be especially blessed by their god. They want to be heroes and **martyrs**: people who die or are put to death because of their beliefs. They are not afraid to die, in fact they are happy to do so. Sometimes they wish to become suicide bombers because a member of their family has been killed and he or she wants to take revenge. Their families will often be given money and special treatment by the leaders of the group.

14. Why do we say someone is a lone-wolf terrorist?

A lone wolf is a wolf that hunts on its own and not with the other wolves in the pack. A terrorist is called a lone wolf if he (or she) carries out a terrorist act alone or with just one or two others. In fact this kind of terrorist is usually male. He may like the ideas of a terrorist group, and wants to copy what it does. He may have read about it online, and he wants to win the approval of the group leaders. Sometimes the lone wolf isn't a terrorist; he is just a person full of hate for the world or for a particular group of people. He may be ill or very angry and sad. What he does may not be called terrorism; it may be called hate crime.

See Q18. Who is a terrorist? (p 54)

15. Why can terrorist attacks not be stopped before they happen?

The police and all the people who keep us safe are working very hard to stop attacks from happening. But they cannot watch every single person who might carry out a terrorist act. Terrorist attacks come as a surprise. Terrorists usually keep their plans a secret and don't tell anyone when they are going to attack. If the police think someone might be planning an attack they will watch and follow that person all day, every

day. But it takes 20 police officers to watch a person for 24 hours a day. They have to take rests and meal breaks; they have to sleep. The police can't watch all the people they would like to. And they can't arrest someone without a good reason.

See Q20. Who is keeping us safe in Britain? (p 57)

16. Why should we be careful who we talk to on social media/Internet?

It's easy for people to tell a story on the Internet and social media about who they are and what is happening in the world. It's impossible for us to know who they really are and if they are telling the truth. They can invent or twist a story. When we go to the cinema or watch a film on TV we watch a made-up story. We know it has been invented. We know the difference between *fact* and **fiction** – stories that are true and stories that are made up. On the Internet and social media it's quite difficult to discover whether a story is true or not. Sometimes we find a lot of *opinions* but not many facts. The storyteller may pretend that a story is true when it isn't. We may only be hearing one side of the story. The person might be telling us a pack of lies. Sometimes the people who write stories and send messages online are very clever. They can make us believe they are our friends. They seem to understand us, our feelings and our problems. They have been specially trained to do this. We must be very careful not to trust people whom we do not know in person. We must protect ourselves against people who want to trick us.

fiction: made-up stories, stories that are invented

Fact and opinion game

Ask the children to write on cards five opinions and five facts. Shuffle the cards and invite each child in turn to pick up a card. When they read the card, they have to declare if it is a fact or an opinion. Encourage them to come up with humorous examples.

Suggest how easy it is to invent a false story when facts and opinions are mixed. We can see this when we look at products. Invite the class to use PCM4 (p 106) to highlight/mark in two different colours the statements which they think are facts and opinions. Invite the children to design their own product and write fact and opinion statements as a follow-on activity using PCM5 (p 107).

Who?

17. Who's who in this book? (An easy reference)

We introduce some important names in this book. Each person or group helps us to put a piece into the jigsaw of understanding terrorism.

See Q36. When did terrorism start? (p 88)

The Assassins *lived a thousand years ago; they believed they had a duty to use violence to protect their community.*

Julius Caesar *was murdered by people who had been his friends. They killed him because they were jealous of his power and wanted power for themselves.*

Guy Fawkes *tried to blow up the King and Parliament because he and other members of the Gunpowder Plot thought the laws in England were very unfair to Catholics.*

See Q29. How does terrorism start? (p 73)

The Suffragettes *used violence and were called terrorists one hundred years ago. Today many people think of them as brave women and admire their struggle for the right to vote.*

See Q33. How can we change things we don't like? (p 81)

__Mahatma Gandhi__ and __Dr Martin Luther King Jr__ both said that using violence was always wrong, even though their communities had suffered very unfair treatment and violence.

See Q27. Where can we see that peace has won over terrorism? (p 68)

__Nelson Mandela__ was sent to prison for 27 years for being a terrorist leader but later he helped to bring peace and democracy to South Africa.

See Q38. When will terrorism end? (p 92)

__Dr Desmond Tutu__, who was Archbishop of Cape Town, South Africa, fought peacefully to end the unfair rule of apartheid. When it was over he brought together the victims of violence with those who had carried it out.

See Q35. How can anything good ever come out of terrorism? (p 85)

__Malala Yousafzai__ was a victim of terrorism but now she fights for peace and for the right of all children to have an education.

18. Who is a terrorist?

typical: average, of a usual kind

There is no **typical** terrorist. You can't recognise terrorists from how they dress or how they look. They could be tall or small, with long hair, short hair or no hair. They don't look different to the people that we pass in the street every day. A terrorist can be male or female, a teenager or an older adult. But there are more male terrorists than female, and they are generally quite young, between 18 and 35 years old. We may occasionally see a photo of a child with a gun or a knife under the flag of a terrorist group. A child can be made to use violence. But children cannot be terrorists. If they are involved in terrorism, it's because adults have forced them to take part. This is a very serious crime. It is also against international law. The United Nations Convention on the Rights of the Child says children should never be used as soldiers.

See Q28. How do laws protect children around the world? (p 72)

Some people say that all terrorists are 'crazy' or 'mad'. Most of the time, it's not the case. Terrorists are often clever at hiding what they really think. But there are people called 'lone-wolf terrorists' who are not part of a group. Among them we may find people who have had very bad things happen in their lives, or who have problems with their thinking, emotions or their behaviour. They may not be terrorists at all. What they do is sometimes called hate crime, not terrorism.

See Q14. Why do we say someone is a lone-wolf terrorist? (p 50)

It can be difficult to tell the difference between a hate crime and a terrorist crime. The same crime can be called terrorism *and* hate crime. One difference is that terrorists usually have a set of ideas that are very important to them. They have plans for the future involving other people. These ideas are bigger than their own hate and anger. People who commit hate crimes often don't have any particular plans for the future. They don't always have a message for politicians or the government. They are not necessarily trying to change what the government or important people do. Their anger is their own anger; they don't always share it with other people.

We could say there are three different aspects of being a terrorist:

- *the person* who feels anger and hatred and wants to take revenge for something not being fair
- *the group or community of people that the person belongs to*, or feels a part of
- *the ideas and goals that the person and the group share*

These ideas and goals are sometimes religious beliefs, but often they are not. For example their goal might be to have a homeland where they can rule themselves. The ideas and goals usually involve a set of rules for living in a different way, with different people in charge.

Invite children to devise artwork around the three aspects of being a terrorist, for example: a circle showing an individual in the middle with a lot of people around them and on the outside something to represent ideas and goals.

19. Who do terrorists attack?

Terrorists attack different groups of people, and for different reasons. There are two main groups: one group is called the **target**; the other group is called the **victims**. The target is usually a government or a powerful and important group. The victims are the people who are killed or injured in an attack. The target and the victims usually belong to the same country. For example terrorists may carry out an attack in a particular country because the government of that country does things the terrorists are angry about. Members of a government usually have bodyguards and are well protected. Ordinary people are easier to attack, so terrorists choose the ordinary people in that country as their victims. Terrorists want to frighten the government and the ordinary people. They want to punish the government and take revenge for the things they don't like that the government has done.

target: the main goal or object (that is attacked)
victim: someone who is hurt or killed (for example in a terrorist attack)

Invite children to think about a different activity that has victims: bullying. Ask them why people bully and how they choose their victims. What can children do to stop this behaviour?

There are various reasons that terrorists choose their victims:

- terrorists want to frighten a government that they hate
- terrorists attack behaviour they hate
- terrorists attack particular individuals whom they hate

Terrorists want to frighten a government that they hate

Terrorists often carry out attacks because they are angry with the government of a country. They want to punish the government for doing things that they hate and they want

to frighten it into doing things differently. The terrorists often know nothing at all about the victims. They are often ordinary **civilians** – innocent men, women and children going about their daily lives. But terrorists don't think of their victims as innocent. For terrorists, civilians are also the enemy. They voted that government into power. (And even though children cannot vote, they are children of their parents, and therefore they belong to the enemy.)

civilians: people who are not members of the armed forces

Terrorists attack behaviour they hate

Sometimes the victims are people whose behaviour the terrorists don't like. This behaviour could be men and women enjoying being together, eating and drinking together, going to a concert or a football match. Some terrorists think this behaviour is **corrupt** – wrong and wicked. They want to punish the behaviour. They want to show that this kind of behaviour is against religious rules. They think that the government should not allow it. They want the government *and* the ordinary people in a country to change their behaviour.

corrupt: dishonest, wicked

Terrorists attack particular individuals whom they hate

Terrorists don't just attack people they don't know. Sometimes they choose their victims carefully and attack them deliberately. They may have a particular reason for hating certain people. For example they might attack a member of the government. The politician might have done something that made the terrorists particularly angry. The politician is then both the victim *and* the target.

EXAMPLE

Charlie Hebdo attacks

Sometimes terrorists choose their victims for particular reasons. They know exactly who they are. This was the case with the *Charlie Hebdo* attacks. In January 2015, terrorists attacked the office of a magazine called *Charlie Hebdo* in Paris, killing 12 people. Several times the magazine had printed cartoons that showed the Prophet Muhammad. The cartoons made fun of the Prophet and of Islam. The magazine also made fun of other religions and printed rude cartoons of many important people. It is against Islamic law to draw pictures of the Prophet, and many people thought this was very disrespectful. In this case the terrorists chose the victims deliberately. They knew the names of the people who worked for the magazine and they wanted to take revenge. Five of those killed were cartoonists. Another victim, killed outside the building, was a Muslim police officer who was on duty. He was killed too although he had nothing to do with the magazine.

People vote for a government and governments make laws that are approved in parliament. Ask the children to complete the sentence: If I could vote, I would vote for someone who... (for example) has done good things for my community.

Or ask them to complete the sentence: If I could change society, I would make it more... fair, tolerant, generous...

Invite children to think of one new law that they would like to bring in. What would it be? You could also encourage humorous examples, such as 'promised to make school holidays longer.'

20. Who is keeping us safe in Britain?

Safety and security

Many different people in Britain help to look after us and keep us safe. The people who have most to do with keeping children safe are *parents and carers*. They provide children with a home, food to eat and clothes to wear. They must also make sure that children from the age of five have a proper education, either at home or school. These duties are set out by law.

School leaders and teachers are responsible for looking after children during school hours. They have very important rules for looking after children which are called 'safeguarding' rules. These rules are there to protect children from any harm that might come to them.

The police carry out patrols in our towns and cities and in the countryside. Police forces all around Britain work together to share what they know about criminals and to prevent crimes like terrorism. If a crime is committed, they also find and arrest the criminals.

It is impossible to protect places like train stations and airports completely because thousands of people walk through them every day. But police are on duty in these places all the time, and there are special police forces for different kinds of transport. Their job is to watch out very carefully for people who might be carrying weapons, or who might put down a bag or a suitcase with a bomb in it. Passengers are told to stay with their bags at all times. The suitcases of all airline travellers are checked by X-ray machines. Passengers have to walk through a metal detector that can detect explosives or guns. Airport workers have a special badge with their name and photo on it. Everyone who works on or with aircraft is very carefully checked.

Britain has extremely strict laws that do not allow people to buy guns unless they have special permission to do so. Criminals sometimes manage to get weapons anyway but this happens less often in Britain than in other countries. This is because Britain is an island nation. The sea makes it more difficult for criminals and weapons to arrive from other countries without being noticed. *Police and customs officers* watch our airports, stations, ports and harbours very carefully. They patrol our borders to stop criminals from bringing drugs, guns and explosives into the country. They often use specially trained dogs to do this.

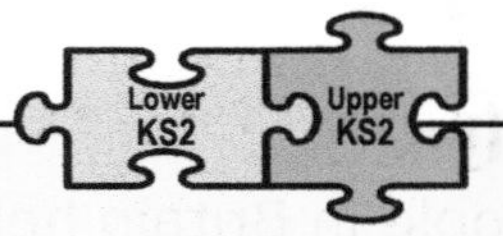

True story

Super hound Brewster – No ordinary dog!

www.watfordobserver.co.uk/news/14212310.Police_dog_Brewster_now_set_to_lap_up_the_good_life/

Brewster is an English Springer-Spaniel. He was born in North Yorkshire but he had so much energy that his owners couldn't look after him properly, so they gave him to the police. Brewster worked for 10 years in a special police dog team with his trainer PC Dave Pert. Brewster's incredible nose led the police to discover large amounts of drugs and weapons. Brewster also helped the police to find and arrest the criminals who were trying to hide them. Brewster retired from the police force at the age of 13. PC Pert said he would be spending his retirement at home, enjoying all his favourite hobbies like chasing tennis balls, swimming in rivers, eating dog treats and napping.

Invite children to read the story of Brewster on computers. Brewster has a special set of skills or qualities. What are the most important things Brewster had to learn? How do you train a dog like Brewster compared to a pet dog?

Ask the children to design a poster showing the different groups of people who keep them safe. This could be used as a focal point on a display wall.

As children read the article, ask them to make notes of the roles Brewster had. Either as a PowerPoint presentation, or as a piece of writing, ask the children to create 'A day in the life of Brewster'.

Ask the children to write down all the people in society who keep them safe, and explain how they achieve this. If possible encourage children to invite a representative from one of these groups into school to discuss his/her role.

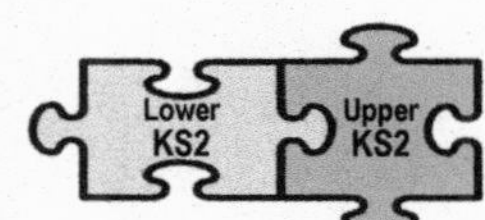

There are security cameras on many streets and on public buildings, shops and banks. *Security guards* keep a watch on these buildings too. If someone tries to break in or commit a crime, cameras will record the scene. Police will study the film later to see who the criminals are.

Britain's *security services* are also very important for keeping us safe. These organisations are not the same as the police. The people who work there don't wear uniform, so we do not recognise them on the streets. They work more secretly and don't talk about what they do. The job of the security services is to protect Britain from all kinds of attack, including terrorism. They are sometimes called 'intelligence services'. This is because they use technology and information in a clever way to discover secret threats and dangers to Britain. They try to stop criminal plans and plots before they are put into action. They don't wait for a crime to happen and then investigate it.

Britain's armed forces – the British Army, the Royal Navy, the Royal Marines and the Royal Air Force – are also involved in protecting us. They have planes, helicopters, submarines, ships and land vehicles. They also have powerful radar and electronic equipment. With all this equipment, the armed forces can detect threats to Britain, even if they

The army has powerful helicopters that help to keep Britain safe

come from faraway countries. Occasionally soldiers are used to patrol airports or guard special buildings.

Partners in other countries also help to protect us. Police and customs officers in Europe, the United States and as far away as South America and Australia share information about criminals and their plans with their British colleagues. If they think that terrorists are travelling to Britain they will tell their British partners, who will be ready. The terrorists will be arrested either before or as they arrive in Britain. British security services and armed forces also work together very closely with partners in other countries.

In Britain many thousands of people are looking after us every day and night, every day of the week, even though we don't know who they are and we can't always see them doing their job.

21. Who are Al-Qaeda and Islamic State?

Al-Qaeda is the name of the terrorist group that carried out the '9/11 attacks' in America in 2001. The attacks are called that because they took place on 11 September.

> ***Teacher's tip***
> *This question may not arise, and the answer almost certainly provides more information than your class will need. The aim is to ensure you have the background and the confidence to respond to questions should they be asked.*

Islamic State was once a part of Al-Qaeda, and was called Al-Qaeda in Iraq. Nowadays Al-Qaeda and Islamic State are separate organisations, though they share many of the same *goals*. Islamic State is called by other names, which are: ISIS – Islamic State in Iraq and Syria; *Daesh* (its name in Arabic) and ISIL – Islamic State in Iraq and the Levant. (The Levant is a name for the countries on the eastern shores of the Mediterranean Sea.) TV journalists often call it 'so-called Islamic State'. They say that because they don't want to show respect for the organisation. They don't want to talk about it as if it is a separate country.

Islamic State is not a country, though it would like to be. It has an army that fights in Syria and in Iraq to win territory. In

these countries it is fighting against the national armies of Iraq and Syria. Thousands of young men have gone to fight with Islamic State from other countries. They are known as 'foreign fighters'. Some families and young women have also gone to live in areas of Iraq and Syria controlled by Islamic State. There are terrorist groups in other countries around the world that say they belong to Islamic State. They say that because they share its ideas. Some individuals who share these ideas have also carried out attacks in Europe – in Paris (France) and in Brussels (Belgium) for example.

Islamic State has a clear set of ideas and goals. It wants to have all Muslims in Iraq and Syria living together in a community called a **caliphate**, ruled by a religious leader called a **caliph**. It believes that the only law should be Sharia law, which is very strict. The leaders of Islamic State think that people living in countries like the US and Western Europe are **corrupt** – wicked and dishonest. They are angry with Muslims who want to have a western style of living, clothes and behaviour. Islamic State thinks that the West wants to destroy Islam. It hates western governments because they sent armed forces to invade Afghanistan and Iraq, which are mainly Muslim countries. Islamic State also considers Israel as an enemy and has attacked Jewish targets. This is because it has taken over land that they say should belong to Palestinians. (There are other people who think this too, but have nothing to do with Islamic State.)

caliphate: the area ruled by a caliph
caliph: a religious and political leader
corrupt: dishonest, wicked

Islamic State hates the governments of many countries where the population is largely Muslim. One reason is that these governments are friendly with the United States and the West. Islamic State thinks that Muslims in these countries do not follow the laws of Islam correctly. Many thousands of Muslims have been killed by Islamic State. It is important to know that by far the greatest numbers of people killed by Islamic State are Muslims.

See Q32. How do terrorists decide where to attack? (p 80) and Q40. If I hear someone say that all Muslims are terrorists, what should I say? (p 96)

Where?

22. Where does terrorism come from?

Terrorism has no 'home'. Terrorism can happen anywhere in the world. It does not 'belong to' or 'come from' any country or any population. Terrorism comes from people, who can be living anywhere. It grows out of very strong feelings of anger and hatred, and feelings about **injustice** – the idea that 'things aren't fair' and someone has to be blamed. The terrorist wants to take *revenge* on the people he or she blames for things not being fair. And that revenge comes in the form of violence. We always think of terrorists as people who attack us. But – and this may seem strange – terrorists usually think that *they* are the ones being attacked. They think they are defending themselves or their community.

injustice: unfairness

For example, see Guy Fawkes and the Gunpower Plot in Q36. When did terrorism start? (p 89)

With terrorism there is always a *story* that people believe in. The story is one of injustice and anger. It has heroes and villains. The story is about **grievances**: anger that unfair things have been done and have not been put right. The story tells of how unfairly a community has been treated, how it has been made to feel worthless and unimportant, how its rights have been stamped on. The heroes are the storyteller's community; the villains are the people who are blamed for the unfairness. They are the enemy. Stories about hate, anger and the wish to take revenge are passed around between people. Sometimes they are passed down through families over generations; or between family members. At other times the stories are shared with friends, or groups of people who share the same feelings. Most of the time people who have grievances try to change things peacefully. But some storytellers want to stir up hatred and anger. They may be in the local community or they may live in far-away countries. They send messages telling people why they should be angry, and why they should use violence. Some of the messages may come on the Internet or social media. The storyteller may be a very powerful speaker, or may send strong messages on the Internet. The message says you have to 'do your duty' and 'defend your community'.

grievances: feelings of anger that wrong things have not been put right

Upper KS2

You also might very occasionally receive messages that try to stir up hate. The messages try to change how you feel about yourself and about people around you. Bullying can happen this way. Sometimes children get together and decide to bully another pupil. It's important to say no to these messages and to tell an adult if you receive them.

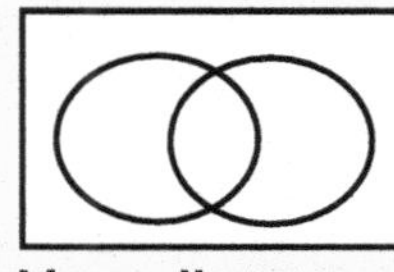
Venn diagram

Give the children an A4 sheet with a Venn diagram. The title is 'My influences'. Ask them to write their name in the middle. On one section, ask the children to write down 'people around me' and on the other, 'technology influences', ie from Internet/social media networks. Ask the children to complete the Venn diagram for themselves. Ask them to then consider how these influences form their opinions and the way in which they respond to a news story. How would they protect themselves from violent messages?

23. Where do terrorists live?

Terrorists mostly live in far-away places. Just occasionally they may live in towns and cities in Britain. If they are members of a local community someone in the area will probably learn about their plans and tell the police. Or the police and other people who keep us safe will discover them before they can do any harm.

See Q20. Who is keeping us safe in Britain? (p 57)

24. Where do terrorists go if they change their minds?

A person – let's call him Sak – decides that he wants to leave Britain and go abroad. Sak is very angry. He thinks his community is being treated unfairly. He wants to fight for a new homeland for the community he belongs to. That means killing or sending away all the people in that area who don't agree. He believes he can help to make a great new life for himself and his community. He thinks that joining a fighting group will be exciting and that he will be a hero. He certainly doesn't call himself a terrorist. He has great hopes of what he and the group can do. But after joining, Sak gradually discovers that being a fighter is quite different to what he expected. The great ideas he had turn out to be a big disappointment. He was expecting to feel thrills and excitement, but actually he

feels afraid all the time. Then he finds that his companions are not the good and fine people he thought they were. They're always fighting among themselves. Each of them wants to be 'top-dog'. They make money out of people who are poor and don't have enough to eat. His companions treat girls and women very badly, and beat them. He wouldn't like his mother or sister to be treated like that.

What can Sak do? He has to leave the group if he can. It's very difficult, and he risks getting killed. But he risks getting killed every day anyway. He manages to escape and get back home. He is arrested at the airport when he arrives and is sent to prison. He wants to make people realise that he made a mistake. He admits that he has done some very bad things, but he is sorry and would like to make things better. While Sak is in prison he has long talks with the staff. They believe him when he says he is sorry, and that he wants to stop other people from making the mistakes he made. Much later, when he comes out of prison, he finds a job as a gardener for the local council. Every week in his spare time he goes round schools and colleges with a police officer. He talks to other young people about what happened to him. He tells them what life is really like when you join a terrorist group. And he tells them not to believe messages on the Internet and social media that say how wonderful it is to be a fighter.

25. Where are we safe?

We can feel safe at home and when we are in school or doing school activities because in these places people are looking after us and making sure we are protected from danger. If we follow simple rules we are usually safe in our home towns. For example we must always look both ways before crossing the street. We wait for the green man to show at traffic lights, otherwise we risk being run over. When we go shopping or to the cinema or for a day out with friends and family we are nearly always safe. It is impossible to guard everywhere in the whole country, but Britain is a very safe country to live in. Our community leaders look out for us too; they want to keep the streets, shopping centres and parks safe for everyone. There are also many thousands of people whose job it is to keep us safe. They work day and night, every day of the week to do this.

See Q20. Who is keeping us safe in Britain? (p 57)

Invite the children to discuss with a partner the places where they feel most safe and secure.

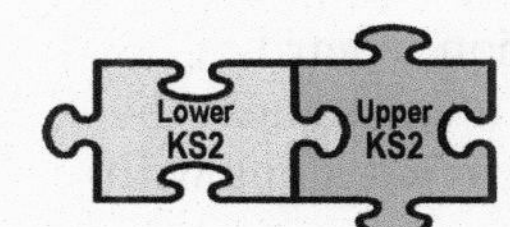

Ask the children to draw a picture based on the theme of 'Safety is...'. The children could have several images depicting those places where they feel safe and secure.

Alternative activity – invite the children to write a poem entitled, 'Safety is...'

26. Where do British values come from?

British values are things that we value – that we hold very dear. We could say they are the best things about life in Britain, the things that make us feel grateful to live here. When we talk about British values we usually mean the *rights* and *freedoms* that British people have. These include:

- the right to live our life the way we want without anyone interfering (as long as we obey the law)
- the freedom to practise the religion we want, or no religion
- the freedom (as adults) to go anywhere in the country we like, whenever we like, with whomever we like
- the freedom to have an opinion, and to write it or say it out loud, as long as it causes no harm to other people
- the right to be treated fairly if we are accused of a crime
- equal rights for men and women

Rights and freedoms are important things that we value and enjoy

respect: courtesy, consideration, regard
tolerance: a willingness to accept and to get along with

British values also involve words like **respect** and **tolerance**. This means being happy to accept and respect differences in other people – for example in how they live and behave. It means not minding if they have opinions that we don't agree with. British values are in fact not just British; we find them in many other countries. But we can be proud of them because we feel they are the best of Britain.

Lower KS2 Upper KS2 **Information box**

Where does 'Britishness' come from?

What do we think about when we think of 'Britishness?' Because of our history we have a fantastic mix of different traditions. This is why British people love things as different as cricket, curry and rap music. Many different countries have an influence on how we speak and how we live. British people have always travelled to and lived in other countries, and Britain is home to many people whose families have their roots in other continents. The umbrella over our heads is Britain, but underneath it is a brightly coloured mix of people, languages and traditions.

Every day we use words that we have taken from other languages. It's easy to forget that they come from other countries because they feel like English. We feel we own them. The barbecue was first discovered by Europeans in the Caribbean islands hundreds of years ago. A *barbacoa* was a wooden frame on posts used for smoking and drying fish. The words pizza and spaghetti come from Italy. Yacht comes from the Dutch language. Many words came into English from Indian languages at the time of British rule in India 200 years ago. This is because British people who lived in India didn't have English words for new things that they found there. For example the word bungalow comes from the Hindi word *bangla* – meaning 'house in the Bengal style'. Other examples from India include pyjamas, shampoo and jodhpurs.

Teacher's tip
Bring a kaleidoscope into class or show a picture of one to the pupils.

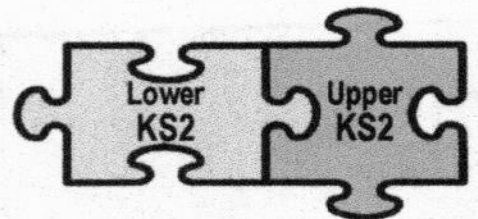

Ask the children to work in small groups (of approximately four pupils) and to study the British values listed on page 63. Invite them to consider how they would explain these values to a) younger children and b) visitors. In their groups, ask the children either to design a poster for their target audience, or to produce a short PowerPoint presentation on British values.

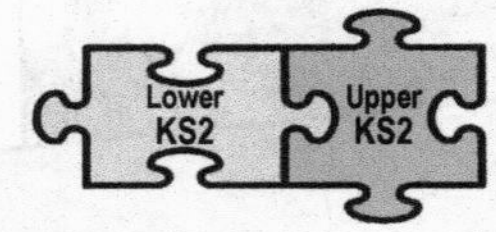

In August and September 2016, 630 individuals represented Great Britain and Northern Ireland in the Olympic and Paralympic Games held in Rio de Janeiro, Brazil. These sportsmen and women competed under the call to action, 'Bring on the Great!' Ask the children to watch a video of the Royals wishing the Olympic team good luck. Invite pupils to discuss the video and to identify five aspects of Britain that make the country unique. What are the different elements that contribute to our brightly coloured mix?

Royals' good luck message
www.youtube.com/watch?v=kplTS3NfQmc#action=share
or
www.bbc.co.uk/sport/olympics/36976827

Each of us has an **identity**. Our identity is made up of all the things that make each of us who we are. That includes our nationality, and the fact that we live in Britain. For each of us, our identity includes things that make us different as well as things we share with others. For example you are part of a family and part of a community in the street where you live. You share your school day with a different community of people. You might share yet another part of your day with people who have the same hobbies as you, or who attend the same mosque or church or synagogue. Who *we* are overlaps with who *other people are* all the time. It's a bit like using Lego pieces. We can all be connected, but we can form different groups. The groups and the pieces can be snapped off and moved around. They can join other groups and break off again. The pieces connect to each other and overlap. Who we are is not just in one group but is shared between all the groups that we belong to. Each of us has lots of different identities.

identity: all the different parts of who a person is

Web of wool

Balls of wool

This activity can be done either as a whole class or with the class divided into groups. One ball of wool will be needed by each group. Give one child in each group a ball of wool. Invite all those who have a brother to raise a hand. The child with the ball of wool passes it on, connecting the children in each group who have their hands up (creating a web of wool). The children must not let go of the wool. Continue the exercise with the wool passing to: every pupil in the group who can say something in more than one language; every pupil who has a relative in another country; who has a cat or a dog.

Continue until everyone is holding a piece of wool. Discuss how membership of each group overlaps with others.

Point out that each group shares something, but that something is also what makes that group different from another one. Suggest all these identities are important and help to make us who we are. They make us different and give us a **common ground** – an area that we share with other people.

common ground: an area where agreement can be found

'A treasure box all about me'

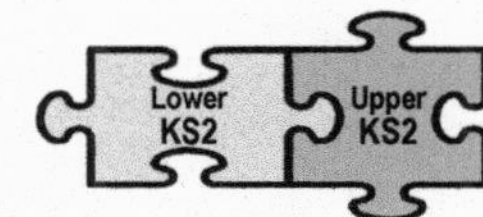

Ask the children to write down a list of things which make them special (as individuals). Encourage them to think about the families, groups and communities to which they belong. Once they have completed their treasure box, invite the children to go through their items with a small group, finding the things they share with other children.

27. Where can we see that peace has won over terrorism?

See Q34. How can we solve a violent conflict? (p 83)

democracy: a country where all adults have a say in how things are run, for example by electing members of parliament

apartheid: 'apartness', the form of government that kept the races apart and unequal in South Africa

South Africa

South Africa has suffered very badly from conflict and violence during its history. For many years there was anger and hatred between different sections of the population. No one could imagine how peace could ever come about. Today, although some problems remain, South Africa is a proud, strong **democracy**. This shows that even the most difficult conflicts can be solved if people really want peace.

For many years South Africa was governed by rules called **apartheid**, which means 'apartness'. The population was divided into four groups: Whites, Blacks, Coloureds and Indians. Only Whites could vote in the national parliament and own land. Most of the native black population lived in very poor areas called homelands. They had to ask permission to go to the white areas, and they couldn't use the same hospitals, schools or even go to the same beaches as white people. An organisation called the African National Congress (ANC) protested about this, and tried to change things peacefully. The South African police and military used a lot of violence against people who protested. Many people were killed. Some members of the ANC decided that it was necessary to use violence to defend themselves and to win equal rights. To begin with they tried not to hurt people; they damaged buildings and machinery. But later on they used explosives and planted bombs that killed people. Terrorism was used on both sides – by the government and by the ANC. One of the leaders of the ANC was Nelson Mandela. During the worst years of violence he was in prison. He didn't kill anyone but he was sent to prison for more than 27 years for being a terrorist leader. Nelson Mandela didn't hate white people; he just wanted everyone to have the same rights. Apartheid finished because the white South Africans realised they couldn't keep it going any longer. Too many people were against them, both nationally and internationally. Nelson Mandela was freed from prison in 1990. In 1994 there was a general election. For the first time adult South Africans of all races could vote for their members of parliament. South Africa became a *democracy* and Nelson Mandela became its first president. South Africa is

called the 'rainbow nation' because of all the different races who belong to it. The country still has many problems. There is a wide gap between rich people and poor people. But the South Africans have tried to put aside their hate and anger and to live together in peace.

See Q38. When will terrorism end? (p 92)

Flags

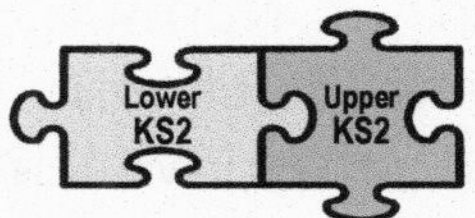

South Africa is called the rainbow nation because of all the different peoples that live there. In 1994, the new South African flag was introduced. It was designed by Frederick Brownell. The flag was a **symbol** of the new-found unity of the nation. Show children a picture of the South African flag. Then ask them to design a new flag to represent all aspects of Britain.

symbol: an example or picture that represents, or is a sign of, something else

South African children enjoying making music together

Upper KS2

Information box

Northern Ireland

Another country where peace has returned after terrorism is Northern Ireland.

The island of Ireland is divided in two parts: in the south is the **Republic** of Ireland, in the north is Northern Ireland. The Republic of Ireland is an independent country with a president. Northern Ireland belongs to Britain, which is a **monarchy**. During the 1960s the Catholics who lived in Northern Ireland felt that life was very unfair. They did not have the same rights to jobs and houses as Protestants.

republic: a nation where the president is elected or chosen
monarchy: a nation ruled by a king or queen

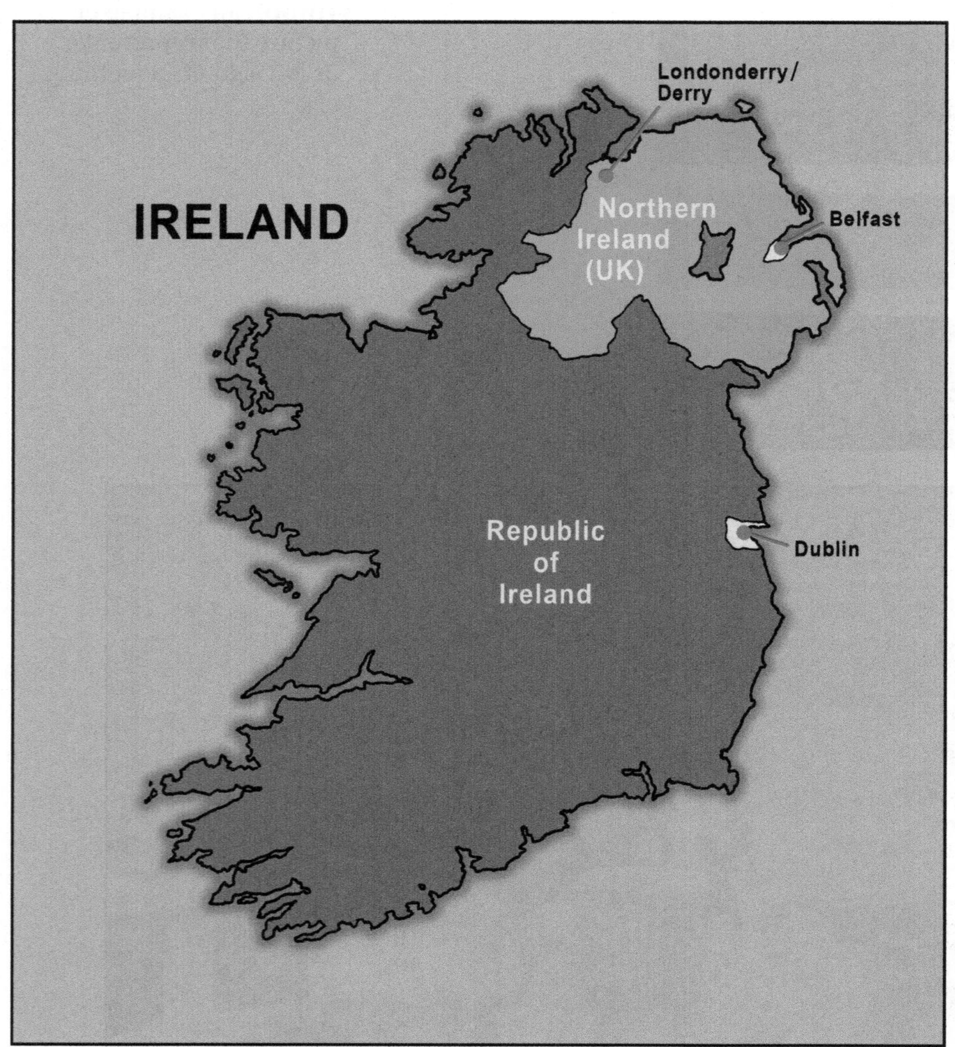

Teacher's tip
Show children a map of the island of Ireland and point out places of interest.

There were many protests about this, and some of them turned violent. Most Catholics in Northern Ireland wanted all of Ireland to be an independent country and not a part of Britain. Most Protestants wanted Northern Ireland to stay as a part of Britain. Catholic and Protestant terrorist groups were formed. The Provisional Irish Republican Army (the IRA) was formed in 1969. Its goal was to get rid of British rule in Northern Ireland. Its members thought that the only way to do this was by using violence. The British army was sent to Northern Ireland to keep order. The army also used violence, especially in Catholic areas. The IRA used terrorism against Protestant groups *and* against the British army.

Teacher's tip
If appropriate, explain that Catholics and Protestants are all Christians, but they follow Christianity in different ways. One difference is that Catholics consider the Pope to be head of the Church, whereas Protestants do not recognise his authority.

From 1969 till 1998 over 3,600 people were killed by bombs and guns. More than two thousand of them were ordinary men, women and children.

After many years the terrorist groups realised that neither side was going to win. The violence had brought great suffering to both the Catholic and the Protestant communities. Very secret talks began between the different groups. They went on for many years. People called **mediators** were a great help. Mediators are people who are not directly involved in the struggle. They can talk to both sides, sometimes together and sometimes separately. In 1998 a peace agreement was signed. It is called the Good Friday Agreement because it was signed just before Easter that year. Terrorists on both sides promised to give up their weapons and to stop their violence.

mediator: someone who is in the middle, who helps other people to find an agreement

In Northern Ireland anger and hate have not disappeared altogether. A very few people still carry on with terrorism. But almost all the population wants to live in peace.

See the Londonderry/ Derry Peace Bridge in Q38. When will terrorism end? (p 93)

A mediator can help to solve problems and make peace

28. How do laws protect children around the world?

See Q20. Who is keeping us safe in Britain? (p 57)

United Nations: an organisation formed in 1945 to which almost all countries belong
Convention: an agreement in international law

Every country has laws that protect children. These are called national laws. There are also important international laws to protect children, made by the countries of the **United Nations**. The United Nations is an organisation made up of almost every country in the world. Its headquarters are in New York. Every year the governments of the countries that belong to it meet together in New York. They discuss the world's most important problems and try to agree on the best way to solve them. When they agree, they write down what they promise to do. The promises are put into agreements called **Conventions**. The Conventions become law in each of the countries that have agreed them. One of these is the United Nations Convention on the Rights of the Child. It says that children have special rights which must be respected, and gives a list of what these rights are. The Convention says that all children have:

- the right to proper healthcare
- the right to go to school
- the right to be protected from harm and cruelty
- the right to have their views listened to, and
- the right to be treated fairly

It also says that governments must not allow anyone under 15, and if possible anyone under 18, to fight in an army. All the governments that have agreed the Convention have a duty to make sure that these rights are respected. Sadly children's rights are not always protected around the world and children suffer as a result.

Child-friendly version of the UN Convention on the Rights of the Child
www.unicef.org/rightsite/files/uncrcchilldfriendlylanguage.pdf

Invite children to look at the child-friendly version of the UN Convention on the Rights of the Child and ask them to highlight the word 'protect' in the document.

Ask them which rights they treasure most. Invite them to design a poster showing the right that they consider is the most important.

29. How does terrorism start?

Terrorism usually starts with someone, or a group of people, with very strong feelings of anger and hatred. They feel that things aren't fair. They feel that wrong things have been done, either to themselves, their families or their community. They blame an enemy for these wrongs. The enemy is usually a government, or whoever is in charge. They think that no one will put the wrong things right. With terrorism there is always a story about unfairness that people believe in. The story may go back a long way in time or it may be a story of life today. It may be a true story; it may be partly true or may be a made-up story. The story makes some people so angry that they decide to use violence.

People who decide to use terrorism feel that they don't have a voice, or that no one is listening to them. They don't believe that the people in charge will change things for the better. They think that the government, or whoever is in charge, does not **respect** their rights or the rights of their community.

respect: courtesy, consideration, regard

It's possible that they may have tried protesting peacefully in the past. But if so, they have decided that peaceful ways don't work, or else they take too long. Terrorists think that violence is the *only* way to reach their goals. It can be very difficult for us to understand the kind of anger terrorists feel because it's so strong. It is so strong that they are ready to kill and to die for it.

Circle time activity

Ball

Pass round a ball or some other familiar object and invite children to recount a fair or unfair situation of their own experience.

Fair/unfair game

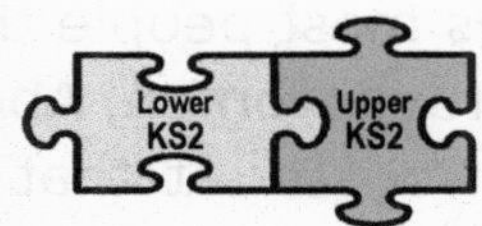

Divide children into small groups, giving each group a selection of eight cards from PCM6 (p 108) with different scenarios. Some are fair, others are unfair. Children take turns at picking a card and discussing whether it is fair or unfair. Adapt as appropriate for age levels.

grievances: feelings of anger that wrong things have not been put right

Terrorism always has a story about unfairness or *injustice*. The story is about wrong things that have been done and not put right. Feelings of anger when wrong things haven't been put right are called **grievances**. Grievances can be feelings of anger about what happened a long time ago or about things that are happening today.

Invite children in pairs to discuss a time when they felt they weren't listened to, when their rights were ignored or when they were treated unfairly. This could be in the context of home or school (rules or decisions made over their heads without discussion) or with friends. Invite them to act out a role-play to explain these grievances. If the grievances were resolved, how was this done? Ask them to make a visual representation of what happened.

discrimination: unfair treatment, or treating people differently for a reason (a reason which is in the mind of the person who discriminates)
prejudice: feelings of dislike or hostility towards something or someone

When we study terrorism we sometimes hear about experiences of **discrimination**. Discrimination is another word for unfair treatment. Discrimination often comes from **prejudice**: feelings of dislike or hostility towards something or someone. Racial discrimination comes from a prejudice against people from a different race. Religious discrimination comes from dislike or fear of people of another religion. Gender discrimination usually means giving more rights to males than to females. For example, men are sometimes paid more than women for doing the same work. Many years ago British women could not vote or be members of parliament. British women who were angry about this formed a group to demand equal rights for women. They were called the Suffragettes. Some people said the Suffragettes were terrorists because they used violence.

Lower KS2 / Upper KS2

Information box

The Suffragettes

Nowadays most people think of the Suffragettes as a group of very brave women. About a hundred years ago they were called terrorists. At that time women could not vote in a general election in Britain or be members of parliament. Many women (and some men too) were very angry about this. They formed a group to protest about it. They were called Suffragettes because they wanted women's **suffrage** – the right to vote. The Suffragettes wanted to send a message to members of parliament that they were angry and wanted things to change.

Teacher's tip
Simplify as appropriate for Lower KS2.

suffrage: the right to vote

⇨

They started by protesting peacefully. Then they found that people paid more attention to them when they were violent. They set fire to buildings, they dropped lighted matches into letter-boxes and they broke the windows of big shops and important buildings. They set fire to cricket clubs and golf clubs that had only men as members; they damaged paintings and statues in art galleries. They sent death threats to the King (George V) and to members of parliament who did not want to give the vote to women. They also damaged churches. This was because most church leaders were against women having the right to vote. The Suffragettes did not want to kill anyone. All the same, some of their attacks caused injuries, and people could have died. The newspapers at the time wrote about 'mad women' and 'dangerous and wicked violence' carried out by 'terrorists'.

By 1914 over a thousand Suffragettes had been sent to prison for weeks or months at a time. There they were treated very roughly. When World War I started in August that year, all the Suffragettes in prison were set free. Most of them stopped protesting. They decided to do what they could to help Britain during the difficult years of the war. Because thousands of men were abroad fighting, many women went to work outside the home for the first time. They did jobs that men had always done: they worked on buses, in factories and in shipyards. In 1918 women were allowed to vote for the first time. People still argue about whether they got the vote because they protested, or whether they got it because they had worked so hard during the war.

Follow this up with a project of your choice on the Suffragettes.

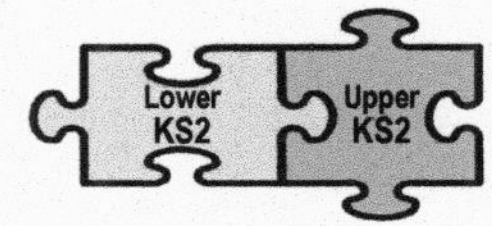

Ask the class whether they think the Suffragettes were terrorists or not. Ask them why they think women won the right to vote.

30. How does someone become a terrorist?

This is a very difficult question to answer. For every single terrorist the answer will be different. People decide to use violence because they feel they have *reasons* for being angry. They think things aren't fair and they want to take revenge on an enemy – the person or people whom they blame for things not being fair. But we don't all feel angry about the same things. And even when we see unfair treatment, for example of people or animals, some of us don't seem to get as angry as others. We all have different ways of dealing with things we don't like, or which make us unhappy.

Seeing Red! Thinking about what makes you angry and why

Ask the children to draw a red circle on a piece of plain paper. Explain that if a person becomes very angry we often say that he or she is 'seeing red'. We also talk about a 'flash point' as the moment when someone loses their temper. Ask the children to write down in the circle things which make them angry. Then ask them to explain why this is so.

When we talk about how people become terrorists, it's important to remember that many people feel angry and many, many people feel that things aren't fair, but only a tiny number become terrorists. We often do not know what each person's reasons are. But we do know that there can be many different reasons. Some of them have to do with who the person is, their personality and character. Some of the reasons come from their own experiences – of feeling unfairly treated, for example. Some of them come from stories of unfairness that they have heard that make them angry. Together, the reasons belong to that person and that person only. Here are some of the things that can have an influence:

- shared feelings
- hatred and fear of another race or religion
- being unhappy, bored or lonely
- bad experiences
- religion

Shared feelings

Some terrorists carry out violent acts alone without any help from other people. More often, terrorists have feelings of anger and hatred that are shared with others. The others might be in the same neighbourhood or town, or they might live in another city or country. People feel surer of themselves when they know that their feelings are shared. Some share their anger and hatred with people they meet online. Others may have friends or a family member who are already in a violent group. They will join because they want to be with their friends, or because the family member has persuaded them. Good friends or family members are more likely to trust one another.

Hatred and fear of another race or religion

Certain forms of terrorism involve feelings of hate for people of a particular race or religion. The people who use violence for these reasons believe that only their own race or their own religion is 'pure' and good, and that all the others are the

> ***Teacher's tip***
> *You may wish to make a comparison here with the Holocaust if appropriate.*

opposite – dirty or bad. They feel *threatened* by people from the other race or religion and are afraid of them. They want to send them away or kill them.

Unhappy, bored or lonely

Some people may join a terrorist group partly because they are lonely or bored. They feel they have nothing to look forward to, and life seems empty. It's easy to think that being a member of a group will make life more interesting. We like the idea of belonging, of being a part of something. For someone looking at a terrorist group from the outside, violence can sometimes seem exciting. The danger can make belonging to the group seem more interesting. When someone has a job to do or a role to play in a group, they can feel useful and important. Young men and women are often tricked into believing that they are fighting for a better future. But if they do join a terrorist group, their ideas often change. They find their new life is disappointing and not what they expected.

EXAMPLE

A Norwegian terrorist called Anders Breivik killed 77 people in Norway in July 2011. Eight of the victims were killed by a car bomb outside the prime minister's office in the capital, Oslo. Most of the other victims were teenagers staying at a summer camp on an island. The camp was run by the political party that was ruling Norway. Anders Breivik was angry because the government was welcoming Muslim immigrants to live in Norway. He said he was trying to protect Christian traditions in Norway. He thought the way of life in Norway was being threatened by Muslims. He wanted to frighten the government: he wanted to force the government to stop welcoming Muslim immigrants and to send them back to their own countries.

Bad experiences

Sometimes people who use violence have an experience of being treated badly or of suffering. Perhaps their families or their community have been treated unfairly. The experience of being treated without respect is called **humiliation**. Being **humiliated** makes a person feel small, without value. It can lead to hatred for the person or people who are blamed for this.

humiliation: the experience of being treated without respect
humiliated: made to feel worthless, unimportant

Religion

Some people become terrorists for religious reasons – they have been told that their religion wants them to become warriors and fight for victory against an enemy. Almost all religions have been used in this way. 'The enemy' is anyone who does not share or accept the religious beliefs. People who are very certain about what they believe can pretend that violence is a good thing. They can imagine that they are doing something fine and brave. But many people who believe this have been tricked. They are often young people who have not studied religious teachings carefully. It's easy to believe people who tell you a story if they have a strong and powerful way of talking.

See Q10. Why do people say that terrorism is about religion? (p 46)

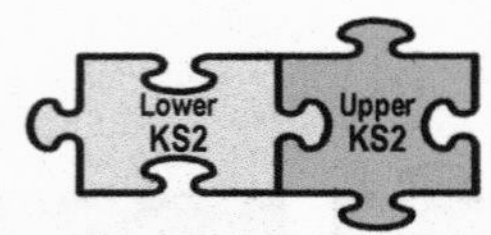

Musical instruments

Some expressive music

Word cards

Invite the children to work in small groups of 4–6. Explain to them that music is often used to represent feelings of love, joy and hope. Music is a kind of story without words. Explain that music can also represent changes in mood. Find some music that expresses strong feelings to use as an example. Using whatever musical instruments are available, invite the children to compose a short piece of music. It should include the feelings of love and peace, moving to hurt and humiliation. Ask the children to agree how their composition will end. Ask them to think about some of the influences already talked about. These key words – shared feelings, hate, fear, unhappy, bored, lonely – might help them with their composition and could be displayed around the room.

Think about the words *push* and *pull*. There are things that push us from behind and there are things that pull us towards them. We are pushed into doing something new because of bad experiences. These bad experiences make us want to change things and get away from what we don't like. At the same time we are pulled by an idea of something better, something good we think will happen if we take a new path. Ideas of push and pull are sometimes used when we talk about terrorism. The push ideas for terrorism are the bad experiences or unhappiness that a person may have had; the pull ideas are the aspects of the terrorist group that the person is attracted to: having an important job to do, belonging to a group, the group's ideas for a better life.

The forces of push and pull are not just used about terrorism. They are often used about people who **migrate** to other countries. Bad experiences like war and poverty push them away from their homes. Hopes for a better job or a safe place to live attract or pull them to a new country.

migrate: to leave one's home for another region or country

See Storyline: Joe Bear (p 97)

Ask the children if they can say which of the above-mentioned influences (shared feelings, etc) may be a push factor and which a pull factor.

Ask the children how they make choices. Invite them to list three things that they don't like, that would push them away from how life is now (for example three negative things). Then invite them to think of three things that would pull them towards doing something new (for example three positive things).

31. How can we stop someone becoming a terrorist?

If you hear someone saying especially hateful things, or if you hear a person say that he/she would like to kill someone or join a violent group you should tell a responsible adult you trust as soon as possible. That adult could be a teacher or a parent or carer. They will know what to do next. It's not your job to get involved more than that. It may be that the person is just feeling angry and is in a very bad mood. Probably the person is not going to become a terrorist at all, but is having a bad time for other reasons. All the same, it's best that you tell someone, preferably an adult, then you don't need to worry any more.

It's not easy to say who the best person is to stop someone from becoming a terrorist, or how this can be done. The people who might be able to help the most – family members – may have no idea of what is going on in the person's head. If someone has taken a decision to join a violent group they often won't talk about it. They know their family will be upset and will try to stop them. Sometimes a mother can persuade a son or daughter to step back from violence. Or else a father

or other family member can help. A teacher, family friend or a faith leader can be involved, especially if there is trust and respect between them. Someone who is angry and full of hate may not want to talk to friends, family or teachers. Then the police can be the best people to help. Police officers are trained to know what to do in this situation. They know experts who have studied these problems for many years. They are not members of the police but are very good at talking to people who are angry. They can often help the person to give up their violent thoughts and plans.

32. How do terrorists decide where to attack?

See Q12. Why do terrorists kill innocent people that they don't know? (p 49)

symbol: an example or picture that represents, or is a sign of, something else

Terrorists sometimes attack people or places that are **symbols** of what they hate and are angry about. A symbol is a sign; it stands for or represents a bigger idea. This is why terrorists attack famous monuments like government or parliament buildings. They want to frighten the government. They also want to frighten ordinary people and make them afraid to go out and travel around. For this reason they attack places which are difficult to protect completely, like busy city centres where people meet up and go shopping.

hijack: to take over a vehicle, keeping the passengers as hostages

See Q21. Who are Al-Qaeda and Islamic State? (p 60)

On 11 September 2001, terrorists belonging to a group called Al-Qaeda **hijacked** four passenger planes. They made two of them fly into the Twin Towers of the World Trade Center in New York, USA. The Twin Towers were a symbol of the United States and its power. The Twin Towers were on postcards of New York. Tourists took photos of them. They were also a symbol of American money: many big banks and important American companies had their headquarters there. The Al-Qaeda terrorists saw the United States as their main enemy. In their opinion the US was fighting a war against Islam and wanted to destroy it.

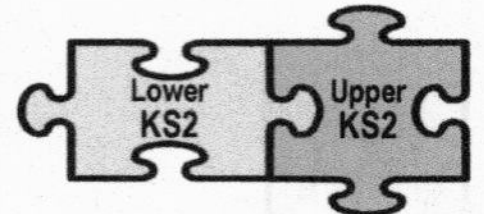

For most of us, symbols are signs of things we particularly admire or treasure. For example a red heart is a symbol of love; a dove is a symbol of peace. The Union Jack is a symbol of Britain. Invite the class to think of symbols of things they know about: their town, county, country or school. Symbols could include particular monuments, landscapes or buildings, or else the school crest as a symbol for all the pupils who go to the school. Invite them to draw symbols of Britain.

33. How can we change things we don't like?

If there is something we don't like or we don't agree with, it's always best to talk about it. We should be able to bring our feelings out into the open in a calm and peaceful way, without being angry. We should try to explain what it is we don't like and why. Then we can listen to the other person's point of view. The other person may have reasons that we don't know about. If we understand another person's point of view then it's easier to solve a problem. We may be able to find an agreement. The agreement may not be exactly what we want, but it may still be better than what we have now. This is called looking for **common ground**. Finding common ground means finding an area that we can share, where we find things that we want and that the other person wants.

common ground: an area where agreement can be found

Steps to peace

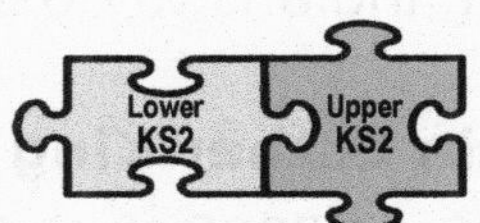

We all have disagreements and fall-outs. These can happen when a decision is made that we don't agree with, or don't like. We have to take steps to resolve the issue. We can think of this as putting stepping stones across a stream. Give the children a sheet of A4 paper with a picture or drawing of a stream. Invite the children to think of a recent disagreement and sketch or write it at one side of the stream. On the stepping stones, ask the children to note down the stages that led to the disagreement being resolved.

Picture of stepping stones over a stream

Finding an agreement often has to be done one step at a time

Lower KS2 Upper KS2

Information box

Changing things in a peaceful way

Here are some examples of people who tried to change things they didn't like in a peaceful way:

Mahatma Gandhi (1869–1948)

Ask children if they have heard of the Indian leader Mahatma Gandhi. He lived in India when India was part of the British Empire. Indians didn't have any **political power** – they couldn't rule themselves. They had to do what the British said and obey laws made by the British. They were sometimes treated badly by the British. Gandhi and many other Indians were very unhappy about this. Gandhi wanted the British to leave India and the Indians to rule themselves. He wanted political power for Indians. But Gandhi didn't believe in using violence; instead he thought that Indians should use **civil disobedience**. He wanted Indians to refuse to obey British laws that were unfair to Indians. Gandhi was arrested and sent to prison many times for disobeying British laws, and for asking Indians to do so.

political power: the power to decide how a community is run
civil disobedience: peaceful refusal to obey laws that are considered unfair
civil rights: rights that all citizens of a country enjoy
discrimination: unfair treatment, or treating people differently for a reason (a reason which is in the mind of the person who discriminates)

Dr Martin Luther King Jr (1929–1968)

When the citizens in a country have what are called **civil rights**, the law treats everyone equally and they share the same rights. Dr Martin Luther King Jr was an important leader for civil rights in the United States. African-Americans in the USA at that time didn't have the same rights as white Americans, and suffered from racial **discrimination**. A group called the Klu Klux Klan thought white Americans were better than blacks and tried to prevent civil rights. Its members carried out violent attacks against African-Americans and people who supported civil rights. Dr Luther King was angry and unhappy about this but, like Mahatma Gandhi, he was totally against the use of violence. He said that although the African-American population had been victims of terrible violence, they should not repay violence with violence. He said,

> *Darkness cannot drive out darkness; only light can do that. Hate cannot drive out hate, only love can do that.*

Dr Luther King won the Nobel Peace Prize in 1964.

See Q38. When will terrorism end? (p 92)

Civil disobedience is still used today by people who use peaceful methods to protest against laws or decisions that they think are unfair. Examples include: farmers who bring their cattle into a busy city centre, blocking all the roads, because they think a law about beef or milk products is unfair; people who refuse to climb down from trees which are to be chopped down to make way for a new road.

Discuss ideas of peaceful protest, civil disobedience and non-violence with the class.

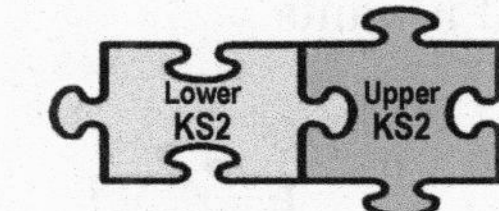

Ask the children to think of examples of being disobedient at home and at school. Why is this different from civil disobedience?

Invite them to organise a peaceful protest about something (at home or school). How would they do it? Find light-hearted examples for this activity, for example lying down in a strategic place to prevent teachers from ringing the bell for the end of break.

34. How can we solve a violent conflict?

The first and most important part of solving a violent conflict is that both sides must really want peace. If one side wants the fighting to go on there is no point in even starting to talk. Conflicts are only solved when both sides want peace and are ready to work hard to find it. The second part is that you need to have brave, strong leaders on both sides who are willing to take risks for peace. If a conflict has lasted a long time it may be very difficult to bring two sides together. They may still have feelings of anger and hatred for each other. Finding a peaceful solution may take many years.

See Q27. Where can we see that peace has won over terrorism? **(p 68)**

When two sides have decided that they want peace, it's important to know how to organise peace talks. To begin with, two enemies may not want to talk to each other directly. If another group has been killing or injuring your own people you probably feel very angry, and it's difficult to talk when you're

See Q27. Where can we see that peace has won over terrorism? (p 68)

mediator: someone who is in the middle, who helps other people to find an agreement
common ground: an area where agreement can be found
compromise: an agreement where each side gives up a part of what it wants

angry. It's often a good idea to find someone else to help. People who stand between the different sides in a conflict are called **mediators**. That means they are in the middle. Mediators are people who can talk to both sides. They don't belong to either side. The important thing is that the mediators are trusted by both sides. Once the mediators have talked to both sides of a conflict, they may suggest a way forward. They may suggest a meeting between the two sides. Or they may suggest that the fighting stops for a while. We call this a 'cease-fire'. If both sides put away their weapons and stop using violence, that can be a good beginning for peace talks. It may take a long time to arrive at this point. The longer a cease-fire lasts the better the chance of peace. If both sides can agree to talk they can look for **common ground**. This is an area where both sides can find things they both want, and which are good for both sides. It might be an *exchange of prisoners*, for example. Then prisoners on both sides are able to go home. If things go well, they may reach an agreement for peace. This will probably be a **compromise**. A compromise is an agreement where neither side gets everything it wants. Each side gives something and receives something in return. Both sides can say that they have won something.

savage (noun): a wild person, someone who does not know how to behave

*I always thought that [building] bridges is the best job there is because roads go over bridges, and without roads we'd still be like **savages**. In short, bridges are like the opposite of borders, and borders are where wars start.*

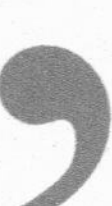

Primo Levi, *The Wrench* 1978

See the Londonderry/ Derry Peace Bridge in Q38. When will terrorism end? (p 93)

Ask children to say what they think this means and why someone might write it. Invite them to design a bridge to peace. Which words would they use to 'build' the bridge (for example tolerance, respect...)? How can we reach out to one another, in our own community and in others?

35. How can anything good ever come out of terrorism?

Terrorism causes terrible suffering in the world. Innocent men, women and children are killed and injured. Their friends and families have to live with sadness for the rest of their lives. But even in the worst experience of terrorism we find people who are kind and brave and generous. Sometimes it can take an emergency to bring out the best in people. People do amazingly good deeds that they might not do otherwise. They risk their own lives to help others. Police and emergency services come to rescue people. This can be very dangerous work. It may involve going into buildings or tunnels where a bomb has gone off, and where there is a risk of more explosions. Ambulance workers move people very carefully and give them first aid. They will talk gently to people who are hurt and then drive them to hospital. Doctors or nurses who happen to be in the area of an attack will rush to help even if they are off-duty. People who live nearby the scene of an attack help too. They invite injured or shocked people to come into their homes to rest or make phone calls.

True story

Stronger together

After the terrorist attacks in Paris in November 2015, Parisians (people who live in Paris) living near where the attacks took place realised that many people couldn't get home. It was late at night and public transport had shut down. People who wanted to help used a Twitter account to offer a bed to anyone who couldn't get home. It was called #porteouverte or open door. Taxi drivers drove people to hospital or to their homes without taking any money. People who are hurt often need to be given blood to help them get better, and for this reason hundreds of Parisians went to hospitals to donate blood. There were so many people that they had to wait for hours, but they waited anyway.

See Q7. What can children do to make the world more peaceful? (p 34)

Parisians waiting to donate blood after the attacks

Sometimes complete strangers become friends and help each other when terrible things happen.

True story

Liz Kenworthy and Martine Wright

Liz Kenworthy (top); Martine Wright (right)

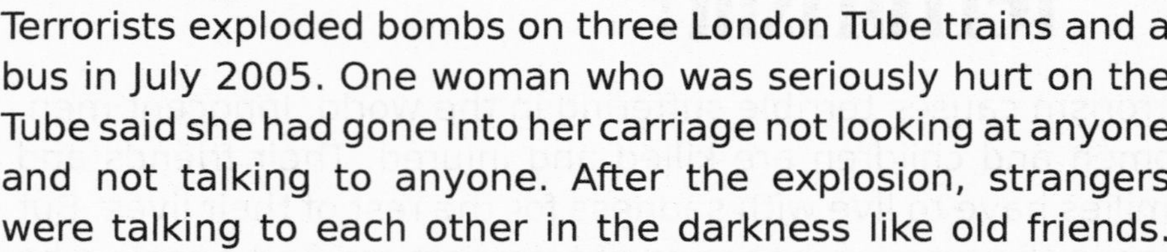

Terrorists exploded bombs on three London Tube trains and a bus in July 2005. One woman who was seriously hurt on the Tube said she had gone into her carriage not looking at anyone and not talking to anyone. After the explosion, strangers were talking to each other in the darkness like old friends.

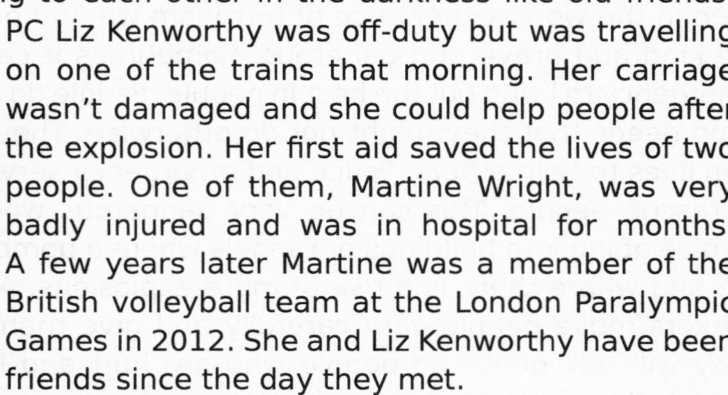

PC Liz Kenworthy was off-duty but was travelling on one of the trains that morning. Her carriage wasn't damaged and she could help people after the explosion. Her first aid saved the lives of two people. One of them, Martine Wright, was very badly injured and was in hospital for months. A few years later Martine was a member of the British volleyball team at the London Paralympic Games in 2012. She and Liz Kenworthy have been friends since the day they met.

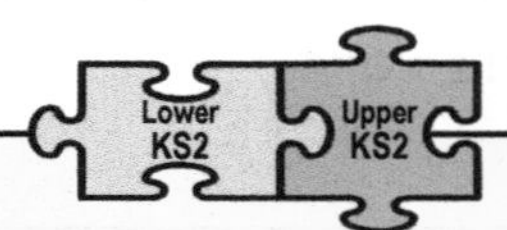

True story

Malala Yousafzai

Malala Yousafzai lived in the Swat valley in Pakistan. When she was 15, a gunman from a group called the Taliban shot her as she was sitting in a school bus with her friends waiting to go home. The Taliban were angry with her because Malala insisted that girls have the same right to education as boys. She had written this in a blog for the BBC and said so out loud many times. The Taliban thought girls shouldn't go to school. Malala was very badly hurt. She and her family were flown to Birmingham where she was given special hospital care. When she was well again she started school in Birmingham. Malala continues to fight in a peaceful way for the education of girls and for women's rights, and has helped girls in many different countries.

She is the youngest person ever to win the Nobel Peace Prize, the most important award for peace in the world. (She shared it with Kailash Satyarthi, who stands up for children's rights in India). She used her prize money to help build a new secondary school for girls in Pakistan.

Malala has shown the world that even a young person can do fantastic things. Perhaps the most important part of her work is her message of peace and forgiveness.
She said she did not hate the gunman who shot her:

⇨

Even if there is a gun in my hand and he [the gunman] stands in front of me I would not shoot him…This is what my soul is telling me, be peaceful and love everyone.

Malala was able to comfort another family that was suffering. Jo Cox was a British member of parliament. She was murdered near her home in Yorkshire in June 2016. Jo's working life had been devoted to helping other people, including refugees from the war in Syria. In her speeches she often said that Britain should do more to help refugees. She was killed by a man who was angry and full of hatred for these ideas. He didn't care that she was the mother of two young children. Malala said that she herself was very small, just like Jo Cox had been, and that like Jo, she often found it difficult to see over the speaker's stand at a conference.

But she showed us all that you can be small and still be a giant. And that's what Jo was – a giant. Jo's message of peace is more powerful than any weapon of war and once again proves that the extremists have failed.

Malala's experience has shown that good can come out of a terrible event. She has helped many other people. She has given people comfort and courage. She has shown other girls that they can stand up for their rights. And she has shown that the way to deal with terrorism is not with more violence but with more peace.

See Q7. What can children do to make the world more peaceful? (p 34)

Malala Yousafzai speaking at the memorial serice for Jo Cox

Invite children to devise a role-play based on bravery or comfort.

Both Malala Yousafzai and Jo Cox made a difference to the lives of many. Ask the children to discuss what difference they would like to make for others.

36. When did terrorism start?

A brief history of terrorism

We don't know exactly when terrorism started, but we know that it is very old. What we call terrorism today – using violence for a reward – has been around for at least two thousand years.

The 'Reign of Terror'

The actual words 'terrorist' and 'terrorism' come from French. They were first used more than 200 years ago (1793–1794) at the time of 'la Terreur' – the 'Reign of Terror' of the French Revolution. At that time, terrorism was used by people working for the government who were called 'terrorists'. They were carrying out the orders of the French government. They deliberately **terrorised** the French people. They used violence to frighten them and make them obey the government's laws. Today terrorism is usually, though not always, violence *against* governments.

to terrorise: to make something or someone very frightened

Here are some examples of terrorism from a very long time ago:

Murder of Julius Caesar

Julius Caesar was a powerful military leader in ancient Rome. He was the highest ruler and called '**dictator** for life' in the Roman Republic. On 15 March 44 BCE, Julius Caesar arrived for a meeting of the Senate, the Roman parliament. Around 200 Senators were present. Caesar had just sat down on his throne when several Senators came forward and stabbed him to death. They had daggers hidden under their **togas**. The plot to kill him involved about 60 people. Many of them had been his friends, but they had come to hate Caesar. They were jealous because they thought he had too much power. They thought one man should not have all the power; they wanted more for themselves.

dictator: a ruler who has great power
toga: clothing worn by citizens of Ancient Rome

Guy Fawkes and the Gunpowder Plot

Guy Fawkes is perhaps the most famous terrorist in British history. He took part in the Gunpowder Plot more than four hundred years ago. The **conspirators**, who were all Catholic, wanted to kill the Protestant King James I of England. They also wanted to kill as many as possible of the English nobles, who were mainly Protestant. The conspirators were angry because they felt that English Catholics were being treated unfairly. They wanted to take revenge on the King for this, and make life better for Catholics. They wanted to place the King's nine-year-old daughter Elizabeth on the throne and make her the Catholic Queen of England. They thought that, being so young, she would do what they told her.

Teacher's tip
If appropriate, explain that Catholics and Protestants are all Christian, but they follow Christianity in different ways. One difference is that Catholics consider the Pope to be the head of the Church, whereas Protestants do not recognise his authority.

conspirator: someone who conspires or makes secret plans with other people
fine: a sum of money that is paid as a punishment for breaking the law
respect: courtesy, consideration, regard
tolerance: a willingness to accept and to get along with
treason: the act of betraying, or being a traitor to one's country

Under the rule of Queen Elizabeth I, who had reigned before James, laws were passed that made life very difficult for Catholics. They could only practise their religion in secret. Catholic church services were not allowed and priests had to go into hiding. Everyone had to go to a Protestant church on Sundays or risk paying a **fine**. English Catholics hoped that King James would show more **respect** and **tolerance** because his mother (Mary Queen of Scots) had been Catholic. But he did not change the laws.

The plotters chose the day when parliament would officially be opened by the King, on 5 November 1605. All the nobles were going to be in the House of Lords that day. Guy Fawkes was discovered very early in the morning, hiding in a cellar beneath the House of Lords. He was guarding 36 barrels of gunpowder, covered with logs. He was arrested and taken to prison. The opening of Parliament did not go ahead that day, but in the evening bonfires were lit around London to celebrate the King's safety. For many years afterwards the fifth of November was a national holiday in England. Guy Fawkes and some of the other conspirators were put on trial. (Others had been killed already). They were found guilty of **treason** (betraying

After Guy Fawkes was caught he was questioned by King James 1

or being a traitor to one's country) and were hanged. Even today, more than four hundred years later, the cellars of the House of Lords are still searched by candlelight by the Yeomen of the Guard on the day before the official opening of Parliament.

The Yeomen of the Guard are the oldest British military unit. The gold and red uniforms date from the time of the Tudor King Henry VII

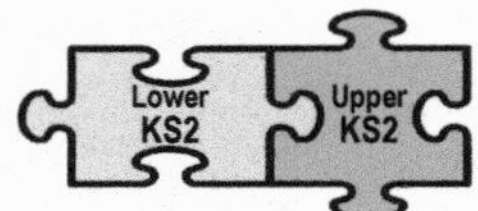

Ask the children to work in pairs and to think of questions they would like to ask Guy Fawkes if they could travel back in time. Ask one child to be in the hot-seat and pretend to be Guy Fawkes. Give several children the opportunity to take this role.

The Assassins

The word 'assassin' is a word we use for a murderer. It comes from the name of a religious group that lived about a thousand years ago in Persia (now called Iran) and Syria. The Assassins felt that their community was being threatened by a more powerful religious group that was ruling at that time. The Assassins felt it was their duty to kill leaders of this group. They felt they had to do this to protect their community and their way of life. Young men were trained to be expert fighters and sent out to kill their victims. They always used a dagger, and tried to carry out their attacks in a public place and on a public holiday. They wanted as many people as possible to be watching. They only attacked the most powerful and important people, they didn't hurt ordinary citizens. Assassins knew they would be caught and almost certainly killed but they did not try to escape. Their wish to have as many people watching as possible is still shared by terrorists today.

See Q1. What is terrorism? (p 24)

Interpretations of the past

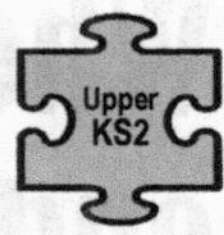

Ask the children to look at the ingredients of the terrorism 'cooking pot' (see p 25). Ask them if any of these ingredients can be found in Guy Fawkes and the Gunpowder Plot. Ask the class to show in a diagram how these ingredients go into the Gunpowder Plot.

37. When will the next terrorist attack happen?

See Q20. Who is keeping us safe in Britain? (p 57)

That's an impossible question to answer. It's a piece of the jigsaw that we cannot find, however hard we look. Everyone hopes there will not be a 'next' attack. Thousands of people are working day and night to prevent attacks and to keep us safe. Because we hear so much about terrorism these days it's easy to imagine that there are hundreds of terrorists in every country, and that a terrorist is hiding around every corner. That's just not the case. In most countries nearly everyone prefers to use peaceful ways of protesting about the things they think aren't fair. Everywhere in the world terrorists, if there are any, are only a tiny part of the population.

None of us knows exactly what will happen tomorrow or the day after tomorrow. In the same way, we can't be certain that there won't be a terrorist attack. Because there are so many people working to keep us safe, we have to trust them and hope they will be successful. If a terrorist attack or other emergency did take place near where you live, the police, your teachers and the adults in your family would look after you. And you can be certain that the police would do everything possible to find and arrest the terrorists. The best thing we can do is to live our lives each day as normal, taking the best care we can of the people and of the world around us.

See Q7. What can children do to make the world more peaceful? (p 34)

38. When will terrorism end?

Terrorism will end when Courageous People work for peace.

Terrorism will end when terrorists get tired of fighting.

Terrorism will end when terrorists leaders are arrested or killed.

Terrorism will end when terrorists, and the people who help terrorists, realise that fighting only leads to more fighting, and suffering to more suffering.

Terrorism will end when terrorists realise that they can't win.

Terrorism will end when terrorists realise that too many people are against them.

Terrorism will end when we build bridges, not walls between ourselves and other people. The bridges can be real or in our heads.

Information box

The Londonderry/Derry Peace Bridge

For a period of almost 30 years, from 1969–1998, more than 3,600 people were killed in terrorist attacks in Northern Ireland. There was anger and hatred between those who wanted Northern Ireland to become a part of Ireland (who were mainly Catholic) and those who wanted it to remain part of Britain (who were mainly Protestant).

See Q27. Where can we see that peace has won over terrorism? (p 68)

Some of the worst violence took place in the city of Londonderry, or Derry. The city has always been divided. It is called Londonderry by Protestants and Derry by Catholics. The River Foyle runs through it, dividing the city in two. Most Catholics live on one side, most Protestants on the other. In 2011 a bridge was built for people to walk or cycle from one side to the other. The bridge has a very unusual shape. It has two high arms which point in different directions, and it has a curvy footpath, shaped like the letter S. It is called the Peace Bridge because it was built to bring two sides together and close a gap over hatred and conflict. It's like a handshake across the river. There are seats on the bridge where people meet friends and chat, or just watch the river go by. It is also used as a place to have fun and celebrate special events like New Year's Eve. Tourists and local people come to the bridge to think about the past and about their hopes for the future. As they walk or cycle across they say something friendly to the people they pass; it doesn't matter whether they know each other or not. The bridge is a symbol of peace and hope in Northern Ireland.

The Londonderry/Derry Peace Bridge – 'a handshake across the river'

Show class PCM7 (p 109), a photo of Londonderrry/Derry Peace Bridge.

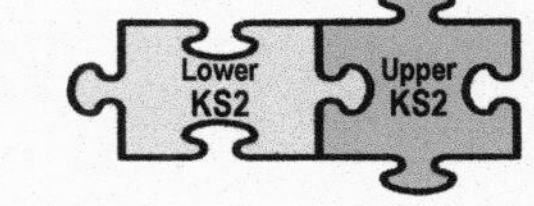

PCM7

Invite children to study the photo of the Peace Bridge, looking in particular at its shape, and discuss with them why it is a symbol of peace.

www.visitderry.com/Peace-Bridge Londonderry-P23773

Courageous People

These are special people who make great efforts to bring peace or help communities to live together in a more peaceful way. Courageous People are people who are good leaders. They are also people who are ready to take risks, with their careers or even with their own lives. But they don't have to be famous or important people. Malala Yousafzai became a Courageous Person when she was just a schoolgirl.

See Q35. How can anything good ever come out of terrorism? (p 85)

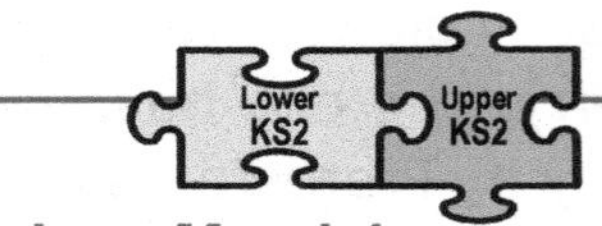

Information box

apartheid: 'apartness', the form of government that kept the races apart and unequal in South Africa

court: a place where decisions about justice are made

wounded healers: people who, because they have suffered a lot themselves, are especially good at understanding other people's suffering and helping them to cope with it

See Q27. Where can we see that peace has won over terrorism? (p 68)

Courageous People: Dr Desmond Tutu and Nelson Mandela

South Africans Dr Desmond Tutu and former president Nelson Mandela (who died in 2013) can both be called Courageous People. Dr Tutu was the Archbishop of Cape Town for many years. He spent much of his life fighting peacefully against the laws called **apartheid**. These laws were very unfair to black and coloured people in South Africa.

In 1984 Dr Tutu won the Nobel Peace Prize for his efforts towards a peaceful solution to apartheid. Later, when the laws were ended, he helped to bring the communities in South Africa together. He was in charge of a special **court**. It was a kind of meeting place for justice, where people came to tell their stories. Families that had suffered violence and torture were invited to talk about what had happened. And the people who had done terrible and violent things also came to tell their stories, often for the first time. When they told the whole truth about what they had done they could ask to be forgiven. Many of them were. Anyone could go into the court and listen, and it was shown on TV each day. Hearing these stories helped South Africans to understand what had happened in their country, and why. Afterwards Dr Tutu said that all South Africans had been wounded by the terrible things that had happened. But he said they were able to help other people especially because they had suffered so much. He called them **'wounded healers'**.

Nelson Mandela spent more than 27 years in prison (1962–1990). He was called a terrorist leader, although he hadn't killed anyone. When he came out of prison he said he didn't hate the white rulers of his country. He said he wanted peace, not revenge. He shook hands with his jailers and started to work for a peaceful end to conflict in South Africa.

⇨

President Nelson Mandela and Dr Desmond Tutu

He won the Nobel Peace Prize in 1993, together with the white South African president who had set him free. In 1994, when South Africans of every race could vote for the first time, Nelson Mandela became the country's president. After so many years of violence and hatred, it was amazing that South Africa could change to democracy in a peaceful way.

Ask the children if they have heard of the Nobel Peace Prize and ask them what it signifies. All of the winners of the Nobel Peace Prize have been 'bridge-builders'. They have looked for ways to bring communities and peoples together. Ask the children in pairs to research one of the winners of the Nobel Peace Prize. What qualities did/do these people have? Which rights did they stand up for/protect? Ask the children to present their findings as a class presentation or as part of a whole school assembly.

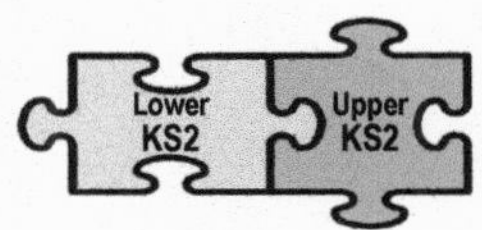

Ask the children when they think terrorism will end. In pairs ask them to come up with three statements beginning, 'Terrorism will end when...' After the children have completed this in pairs, share the statements on a communal board. Ask the class to select one of the statements and turn it into a visual presentation.

See jigsaw pieces on (p 92)

‘If’ questions

Teacher's tip
Questions 39 and 40 have been kept outside the six main jigsaw sections because we do not recommend introducing them unless they are specifically raised. Q39 (If I feel worried...) might arise in the event of a terrorist attack in Britain or elsewhere that makes prominent news headlines. Q40 (If I hear...) may not arise in any form. However, if the question is asked in some form, it is important to state at the outset: a) that terrorism can be carried out by all kinds of individuals or groups and b) that some terrorism has been carried out by Muslims, but that almost all Muslims disagree with it.

39. If I feel worried about terrorism, what should I do?

If you feel worried that a terrorist attack might happen, or upset about one that has happened, you should share your worries with someone close to you. The person could be a parent or other adult in your family, a carer, or a teacher. It's better to talk to an adult as they understand better what's going on in the world. If you find it difficult to say out loud what you're afraid of then you could try to draw a picture, or write your ideas down on paper. Try to work out where your fears are coming from. Who or what in particular is making you frightened? Try to imagine that these are someone else's worries. If you think of them as belonging to someone else it may be easier to talk about them. If you are worried but feel you can't talk to anyone around you, there is a service called Childline which has been specially set up to help children with worries. You can call the Childline number free on 0800 1111 at any time of the day or night. You can talk to a friendly and trustworthy person about whatever is bothering you.

40. If I hear someone say that all Muslims are terrorists, what should I say?

You should say that this is just not true. Most Muslims are certainly not terrorists. Terrorists can be of any religion, or of no religion. There have been Christian, Jewish, Hindu and Sikh terrorists at different times in history. There are at least one thousand six hundred million (1.6 billion) Muslims in the world and only the tiniest number of them are terrorists. Islam does not tell Muslims to go out and kill innocent people. People who say that do not understand Islam. Almost all Muslims want to live in peace with people of other faiths.

Storyline

Joe Bear

A fictional story about suffering and hope for the future

This is the story of Joe Bear, a big and much loved teddy bear. Joe Bear belongs to a girl called Maya. Maya is nine years old and is a **refugee**. She lost Joe Bear when she was seven. Maya and her family had to leave their home because there was fighting in the city and gunmen were hiding in the neighbourhood. It wasn't safe to go out even in the daytime and Maya couldn't go to school. They tried for a long time to stay on in their home. There was no water in the house and her mother had to go each day to collect water from a pipe in the street outside. When her mother came back, her father and brother went out to look for food. There was almost no food in the shops. The family was living on a few tins they had in the kitchen cupboard and some vegetables that they grew in their small garden behind the house.

refugee: a person who leaves home as a result of war or other great difficulty and looks for help and safety in another place

Teacher's tip
The Storyline recounts the misery of violent conflict as seen through a child's eyes. It shows that even after terrible things have happened, peace can come when old enemies are ready to set aside their anger and hatred. They don't have to become friends, they just need to agree not to fight each other any more.

One day there was fighting in their street. Maya's brother was working in the vegetable garden. A gunman shot him from a rooftop and he fell flat on the ground. They had to look after him at home because the hospital had been destroyed in a bomb attack. He wasn't getting any better and he needed medicine so Maya's parents decided to leave the city. They hoped to find a safe place to stay until the fighting was over. They told Maya she could only take a few clothes in her rucksack, but of course she packed Joe Bear too. He is a large bear and he took up a lot of room in the rucksack. Maya's parents told her to take him out and leave him behind. They said they needed to put food for the journey in her rucksack. Maya cried and begged her parents to let Joe Bear go too, but they refused. Maya hugged and kissed Joe Bear goodbye and left him under her bed with a blanket round him to keep him warm. Whispering in his ear, she promised to come back to collect him as soon as she could. With tears running down her cheeks, she left the city with her family.

The family travelled for three days, walking very slowly to support Maya's brother. They found a hospital but it didn't have enough medicine, and he died. At last Maya and her parents reached a border and crossed through to a refugee

camp where they stayed for a few weeks. It was very difficult to live there. It was crowded and dirty and there was no work. Maya's father decided to take the family to a port city where they could find a boat to another country. There he might find a job and Maya could go to school. The sea journey was terrible. There were 30 people in a tiny boat only big enough for 12. Two people fell overboard while they were asleep, and drowned. There was almost nothing to eat or drink. The next day at dawn they saw a coastguard ship coming to rescue them. They were treated roughly but were given water and sandwiches. When they got to land, they were put in a big hut with hundreds of other people. A few days later they were taken to a town where they were given some money. Best of all they were given the key to a small flat near the town centre. Maya's father quickly found a job. Maya started school again but it was very difficult because she had to learn a new language and everyone looked different. Most people were kind but some were rude. They called her names because she was a foreigner and had a different religion to them.

One Saturday afternoon she was out shopping with her mother at the local market. The market sold vegetables and cheese on one side; on the other there were stalls with pots and pans, furniture and clothes. Maya was looking at shoes when she heard a man talking on his phone in a language she recognised, the language of her country. She turned to look round. He was thin and looked very poor. And then, suddenly, who did she see – sitting on the ground with his back against the man's chair – but Joe Bear! She pulled her mother's sleeve and dragged her over to the market stall. 'That's my Joe Bear!' she shouted at the man, 'He's mine! Where did you get him?' Tears of joy and relief poured down her cheeks. She knew it was Joe Bear; there was no doubt about it. He was still wearing the old white pullover her mother had knitted for him years before. And you could see where she had sewn one of his paws back on after a dog had chewed it.

The man looked at Maya sadly. 'Is this bear yours?' he said. 'Really? I found it two years ago and gave it to my son. He was about your age. I was fighting our enemies in the city and we had just taken over that street. I found the bear under a bed in one of the houses. I took it home with me. My son loved that bear. But a month later my son was killed by a bomb. I keep it for his sake.'

⇨

'So YOU were our enemy!' said Maya. She suddenly felt incredibly angry. 'YOU killed my brother and that's why we had to leave the city and our home. 'It was YOUR fault I had to leave Joe Bear behind. Joe Bear is mine! I love him and I want him back.'

Then the man started to cry. He picked up Joe Bear up and gave him back to Maya. 'I'm sorry for what happened,' he said. 'I know I've done some bad things and I'm ashamed of that. We've all suffered so much because of our war – your brother, my son. Do you think we could make peace now? Can Joe Bear be the sign of our peace?'

There was a long silence while they all thought about it. Maya looked at Joe Bear and then at her mother. 'Can we make peace?' she asked.

'Well... I don't know... I suppose so,' her mother replied. We can't be friends, but we can make peace. We have to try to live without hate and without fighting each other. That's our only hope for the future.' Maya hugged Joe Bear and tucked him safely under her arm. Then she and her mother went back home to tell Maya's father the exciting news.

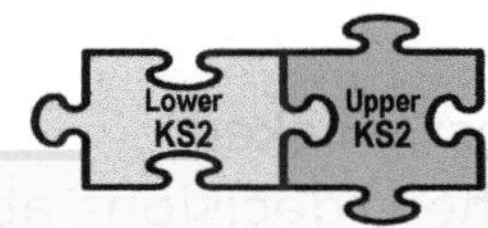

Invite children to depict a scene from the Storyline.

Ask them to make a storyboard with the events described.

Full glossary

apartheid: 'apartness', the form of government that kept the races apart and unequal in South Africa
audience: people who listen to and watch a performance
bargain: an agreement
caliph: a religious and political leader
caliphate: the area ruled by a caliph
civilians: people who are not members of the armed forces
civil disobedience: peaceful refusal to obey laws that are considered unfair
civil rights: rights that all citizens of a country enjoy
common ground: an area where agreement can be found
compromise: an agreement where each side gives up a part of what it wants
conspirator: someone who conspires or makes secret plans with other people
Convention: an agreement in international law
corrupt: dishonest, wicked
court: a place where decisions about justice are made
democracy: a country where all adults have a say in how things are run, for example by electing members of parliament
dictator: a ruler who has great power
discrimination: unfair treatment, or treating people differently for a reason (a reason which is in the mind of the person who discriminates)
diversity: differences, variety
extremist: something or someone that is very different, very strong or very unusual compared to others
fiction: made-up stories, stories that are invented
fine: a sum of money that is paid as a punishment for breaking the law
grievances: feelings of anger that wrong things have not been put right
hijack: to take over a vehicle, keeping the passengers as hostages
hostage: someone who is held prisoner by a person or group of people
humiliation: the experience of being treated without respect
humiliated: made to feel worthless, unimportant
identity: all the different parts of who a person is
infrastructure: buildings, transport and other networks that provide important services
injustice: unfairness
justify: to find or show reasons for doing something
kidnap: to take and keep someone in a secret place against their wishes, usually to make a bargain
martyr: a term used to describe someone who is put to death or dies because of their beliefs
media: TV, radio, newspapers and Internet
mediator: someone who is in the middle, who helps other people to find an agreement
migrate: to leave one's home for another region or country
monarchy: a nation ruled by a king or queen
national anthem: a song to celebrate a country
political power: the power to decide how a community is run
prejudice: feelings of dislike or hostility towards something or someone
publicity: a high level of attention from the public
ransom: a sum of money paid to free a hostage
react: to respond, act as a direct result of something
refugee: a person who leaves home as a result of war or other great difficulty and looks for help and safety in another place

regiment: a large, organised formation of soldiers

republic: a nation where the president is elected or chosen

respect: courtesy, consideration, regard

sacrifice: a gift or offering of great value, usually as part of religious worship

savage (noun): a wild person, someone who does not know how to behave

suffrage: the right to vote

symbol: an example or picture that represents, or is a sign of, something else

target: the main goal or object (that is attacked)

to terrorise: to make something or someone very frightened

terrorism: violence used to frighten people; violence for a reward

toga: clothing worn by citizens of Ancient Rome

tolerance: a willingness to accept and to get along with

treason: the act of betraying, or being a traitor to one's country

typical: average, of a usual kind

victim: someone who is hurt or killed (for example in a terrorist attack)

United Nations: an organisation formed in 1945 to which almost all countries belong

vigil: a watch, a silent standing together of people to remember an event

wounded healers: people who, because they have suffered a lot themselves, are especially good at understanding other people's suffering and helping them to cope with it

Index of names and key themes

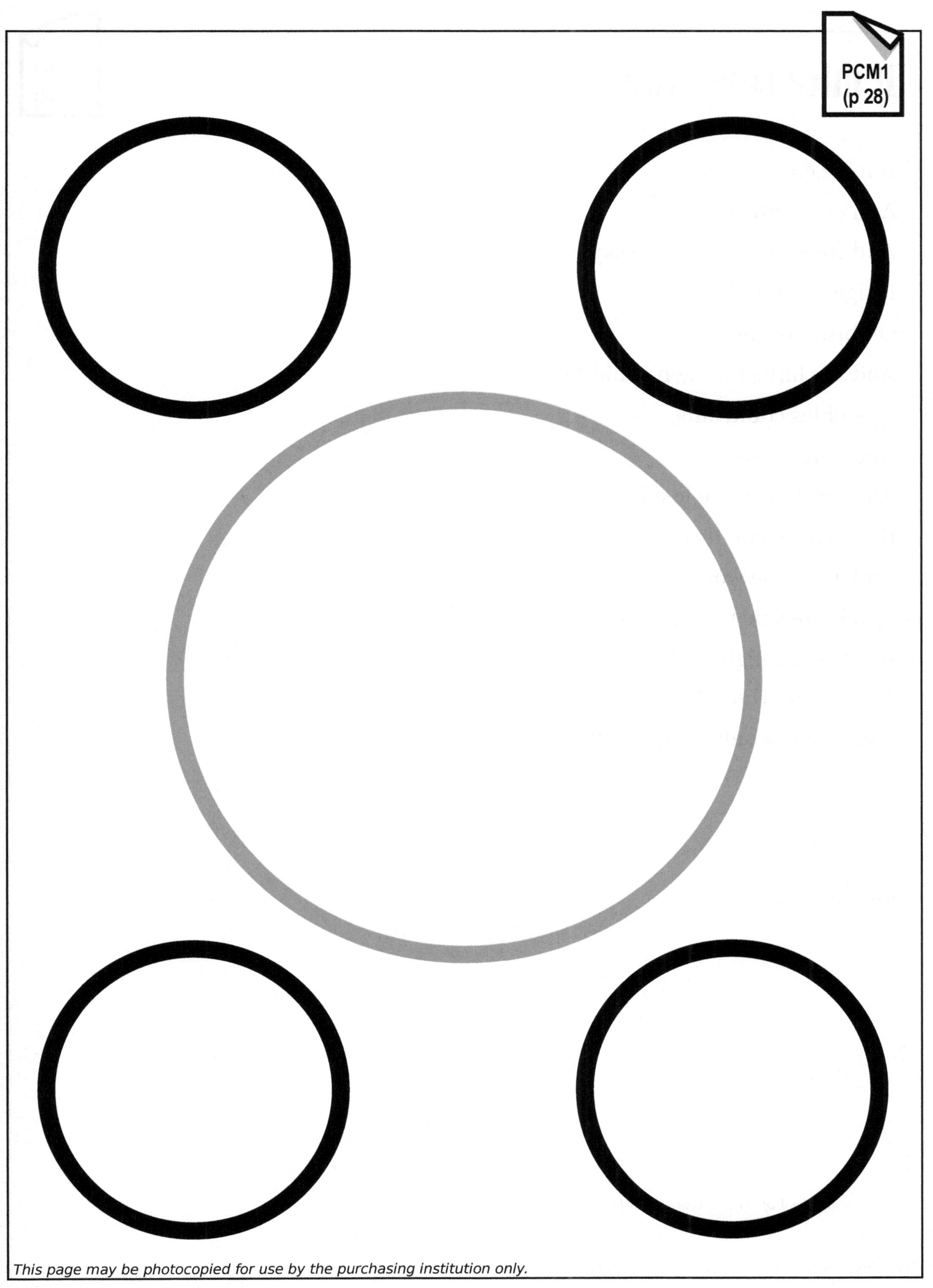
PCM1
(p 28)

If mice could roar

If mice could roar
And elephants soar
And trees grow up in the sky
If tigers could dine
On biscuits and wine,
And the fattest of men could fly!
If pebbles could sing
And bells never ring
And teachers were lost in the post;
If a tortoise could run
And losses be won,
And bullies be buttered on toast;
If a song brought a shower
And a gun grew a flower
This world would be nicer than most!

Ruskin Bond

Ruskin Bond's Book of Verse, Penguin Books India (2007)

True and false cards

Earthquakes and tsunamis are a type of terrorism.	If a person feels terrorised, the reason must be terrorism.	Terrorism just happens, it isn't organised or planned.	Terrorists only want money as a reward.
People are always responsible for acts of terrorism.	Terrorists usually want a reward just for themselves.	Terrorists believe that talking is as good as violence.	Terrorists often feel that something in the world is unfair.
Bullying is a type of terrorism.	Terrorists are often interested in politics.	It would be fair to call a bank robber a terrorist.	Terrorism also exists in the animal world.

Fact or opinion?

- These trainers are absolutely fantastic.
- The cost of the trainers is £39.50.
- World-class athletes think they will help you to run. twice as fast as before.
- You can buy these trainers at: www.reallyfastshoes.com.
- The trainers come in three different colours – red, white or green.
- You will love the trainers so much you want to wear them in bed.
- The British Athletics Club approves of the trainers.
- All your friends will be envious if you buy them.
- Wearing these trainers will help you do your homework quicker.

Can you write three more facts and opinions for this product?

Fact or opinion?

Design your own product here.

Write three facts and opinions about your product and see if a friend can decide which is a fact and which is an opinion.

Fair/unfair scenarios

PCM6 (p 73)

1. A class of 30 children is lined up ready to go into class after break. The teacher asks the children to be silent. All except three children are quiet. The teacher picks out one of the three and says that he/she will lose 5 minutes of their next break. Is this fair or unfair?	2. Two brothers are playing games on a computer at the weekend. Their parents say that they can play one final game before bed. The older brother protests strongly after the game is finished. The younger brother goes to bed quietly. Because of the protest, the older brother is allowed to play another game. Is this fair or unfair?
3. During a class test, the fire alarm sounds. When the children return to class, they are told that they have to finish the test in the remaining time. Children in the class next door complete the test the next day. Is this fair or unfair?	4. It is sports day. The sprint race takes place, but as the children are running, a parent jumps out onto the track, knocking a child over. The race is finished and the winner declared. Is this fair or unfair?
5. Children are auditioning for the school choir. The audition is interrupted as an alarm sounds. The children are asked to come back and audition the next day. Is this fair or unfair?	6. A child becomes unwell during a class test and has to go home. The teacher says the child can redo the test when he/she is feeling better. Is this fair or unfair?
7. A group of six children have fallen out during lunchtime. The argument is mainly between two pupils but the teacher listens to all six children. Is this fair or unfair?	8. It is sports day. The sprint race takes place, but as the children are running, a young child runs onto the track spoiling the race. The race is stopped and the children have a chance to run again. Is this fair or unfair?

Londonderry/Derry Peace Bridge

PCM7
(p 93)

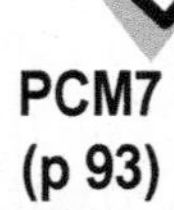

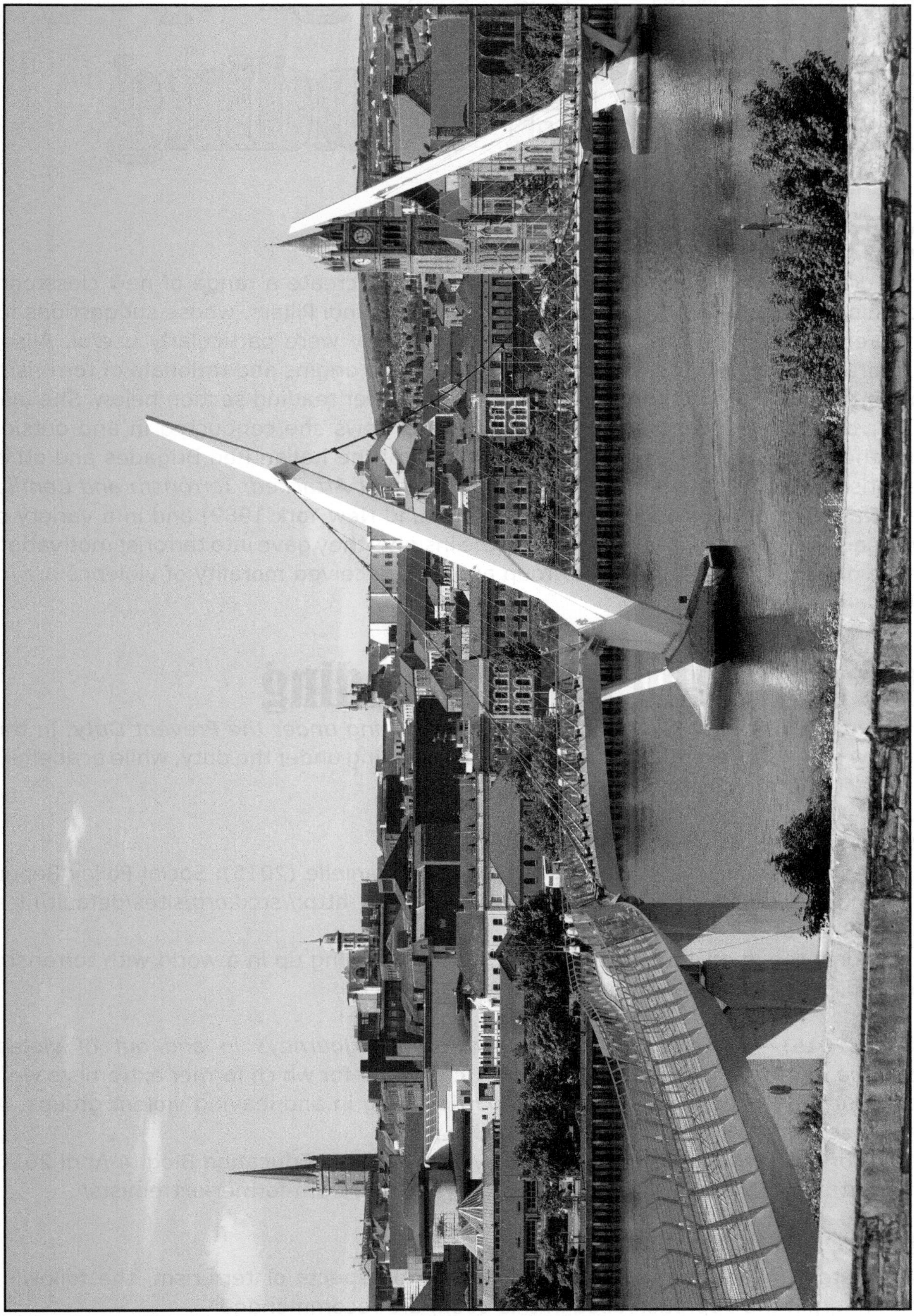

This page may be photocopied for use by the purchasing institution only.

Sources, bibliography and further reading

Sources

Jane Flint has drawn on 14 years of teaching experience to create a range of new classroom activities for this text. Some were inspired by the work of Wendi Pillars, whose suggestions for transforming verbal concepts and ideas into visual imagery were particularly useful. Alison Jamieson has drawn on scholarly research for analysis of the origins and rationale of terrorism, in particular on the work cited in the academic studies further reading section below. She also drew upon her own research and on the extensive interviews she conducted in and outside prison during the 1980s and 90s with leading members of the Italian Red Brigades and other left-wing terrorist groups. These were analysed in *The Heart Attacked: Terrorism and Conflict in the Italian State* (Marion Boyars Publishers, London and New York 1989) and in a variety of academic journals in the following years. Some of the insights they gave into terrorist motivation, the experience of belonging to a terrorist group and the perceived morality of violence are, in her view, still valid today.

Bibliography and further reading

Times Educational Supplement (4 November 2016): *Teaching under the Prevent Duty*. In this extensive review teachers describe their experience of working under the duty, while academics assess the impact of the obligation on schools.

Academic studies, terrorism and children/young people

Garbarino, James; Governale, Amy; Henry, Patrick; Nesi, Danielle (2015): Social Policy Report Volume 29 Number 2: *Children and Terrorism*. Available at http://srcd.org/sites/default/files/documents/spr29_2.pdf
This report explores the impact on children and youth of growing up in a world with terrorism, and considers policy initiatives and programmatic responses.

ConnectJustice (2015): *Formers and Families Transitional Journeys in and out of violent extremisms in the UK*. Part of a multi-country research project for which former extremists were interviewed about their experiences of joining, participating in and leaving violent groups. At http://www.connectjustice.org/UK-Formers-&-Families.pdf
The lead author of this research discusses its relevance at World Education Blog (4 April 2016) https://gemreportunesco.wordpress.com/2016/04/04/learning-from-former-extremists/

Academic studies, terrorism (general)

For those interested in the ideological and motivational aspects of terrorism, the following texts, (which underpin the approach used in this book) are recommended:

English, Richard (2009): *Terrorism, How to Respond*, Oxford University Press, Oxford.
Gearty, Conor (1991): *Terror*, Faber & Faber, London.
Hoffman, Bruce (2006): *Inside Terrorism*, Colombia University Press, New York.
Horgan, John (2005): 'The social and psychological characteristics of terrorism' in *Root Causes of Terrorism: Myths, Reality and Ways Forward* (ed. Tore Bjørgo) Routledge, London and New York.
(Also) Horgan (2009): *Walking Away from Terrorism. Accounts of disengagement from radical and extremist movements*, Routledge, London and New York.
Richardson, Louise (2007): *What Terrorists Want: Understanding the Terrorist Threat*, Random House, London.
Sen, Amartya (2006): *Identity and Violence. The Illusion of Destiny*, Penguin, London. See also Professor Sen in his capacity as Chair of the Commonwealth Commission on Respect and Understanding: *Civil Paths to Peace (2007)* Commonwealth Secretariat, London.

Resources for educators

Davies, Lynn (2008): *Educating against Extremism*, Trentham Books, Stoke on Trent. An excellent text on strategies for use in an educational setting.
Pillars, Wendi (2016): *Visual Note-Taking for Educators: A Teacher's Guide to Student Creativity*, W.W. Norton & Company, New York. This text explains how visual note-taking in the classroom helps pupils to conceptualise and remember key ideas.

Online resources for school use

http://globaldimension.org.uk/glp/page/10757
Offers support to parents and teachers in discussing difficult issues such as terrorism and extremism. The Global Learning programme, 'recommended reading' section is useful, as are several articles on teaching about the conflicts in Syria and Afghanistan. It offers teaching strategies which focus on developing analysis and critical thinking skills.

http://www.citizenshipfoundation.org.uk/index.php
A useful website with many resources on citizenship.
Guidance for schools on the *Prevent* duty can be found at: https://www.teachingcitizenship.org.uk/resource/prevent-duty-and-controversial-issues-creating-curriculum-response-through-citizenship

Oxfam has excellent online resources dealing with global issues at
http://www.oxfam.org.uk/education/global-citizenship/global-citizenship-guides and
http://www.oxfam.org.uk/education/whole-school

http://assemblies.org.uk/index.php
A useful website suggesting topics for a whole school assembly or year group assembly dealing with difficult issues.

https://www.supportrefugees.org.uk/wp-content/uploads/2016/04/In-Search-of-Safety-Unicef-Schools-Resource.pdf
This excellent UNICEF teaching resource for schools explores the refugee crisis and includes learning activities adaptable for age groups from seven upwards.

UK government/parliament resources and references

Two of the most important acts of parliament relating to terrorism in the UK are the Terrorism Act 2000 and the Counter-Terrorism and Security Act 2015. These can be found respectively at: http://www.legislation.gov.uk/ukpga/2000/11 and http://www.legislation.gov.uk/ukpga/2015/6. The government's *Prevent* strategy (2011) is available at https://www.gov.uk/government/uploads/system/uploads/attachment_data/file/97976/prevent-strategy-review.pdf. Objective 3, subsection 10, pp 65–74 concerns schools and children.

The most recent government evaluation of the UK's counter-terrorism strategy was published in July 2016. It can be found at https://www.gov.uk/government/uploads/system/uploads/attachment_data/file/539684/55469_Cm_9310_PRINT_v0.11.pdf

Keeping Children Safe in Education (2016), published by the Department for Education, provides statutory guidance for schools and colleges: https://www.gov.uk/government/uploads/system/uploads/attachment_data/file/550511/Keeping_children_safe_in_education.pdf

Educate against Hate is the Government's principal website for practical advice and information on protecting children from extremism and radicalisation: http://educateagainsthate.com/

Acknowledgements

Our warmest thanks go to all the staff at Brilliant Publications, first and foremost to Priscilla Hannaford for her enthusiasm and for the confidence she continues to show in our writing. Special thanks are due to the Brilliant design team for their imaginative presentation of our book and its themes. They have introduced a visual dimension to the text which greatly enhances its clarity and ease of navigation. We particularly appreciate the help and extraordinary skills of our editor Marie Birkinshaw. It has been a real pleasure to work together. We thank Ruskin Bond and his publishers, Penguin India, for allowing us to reproduce his delightful poem, 'If mice could roar'.

We are grateful to Martin Morgan for reading and commenting on an early draft of this text. Thanks also to Nicoletta Martello, friend and primary school teacher, whose suggestions on what to include in the text were invaluable, and whose invitations to share her lively classroom of 9-year-olds in Castiglione del Lago have been hugely appreciated.

We mourn an enthusiastic follower of our work, Mollie Lang (Jane's great aunt) who died last year at the age of 91. Her lively mind and keen interest in this book continued to the end. Jane would also like to thank all the children she has taught and currently teach. They have inspired her to care more and think more deeply about how we tackle sensitive issues in the classroom. From them she has learned, and continues to learn, so much. Finally our love and thanks go to our families, in particular to husbands Chris and Nigel, who ensured we had the time and space to write and who have supported us heroically.

Biographical notes

Alison Jamieson worked in security consultancy in London before moving to live in Italy in 1984. Since then she has been a freelance writer and consultant on issues of political violence, organised crime and drugs. For her work on Italian terrorism she conducted lengthy interviews with leading members of the Italian Red Brigades and other terrorist groups, both in and out of prison. From 1992 to 1997 she was regular guest lecturer at the NATO Defense College in Rome on problems of international drug trafficking and organised crime. She worked for many years as consultant to the United Nations Office on Drugs and Crime (formerly UNDCP) in Vienna, and was Project Manager and principal author of UNDCP's first *World Drug Report* in 1997. Her book *The Antimafia*, published in 1999, is a comprehensive study of Italy's responses to an upsurge of Mafia violence during the early 1990s. She has written four books on terrorism for the education sector, the last of which, with Jane Flint, was published in August 2015 by Brilliant Publications, *Radicalisation and Terrorism: A Teacher's Handbook for Addressing Extremism*.

Jane Flint is a primary school teacher living in York with 14 years of classroom experience. She has always tried to ensure that important issues of the outside world which affect children can readily be discussed in class. She was teaching in a school of predominantly Muslim children in the Beeston area of Leeds at the time of the London transport bombings in 2005. She was responsible for introducing inter-faith discussions into the classroom in Leeds and arranging for Muslim, Anglican and Sikh faith leaders to visit her classes. She worked as a volunteer in a girls' secondary school in Uganda in the summer of 2007. Jane is responsible for all the classroom activities; her teaching experiences informed and guided the text throughout.

Lightning Source UK Ltd.
Milton Keynes UK
UKOW07f2343260517
302132UK00005B/17/P

9 781783 172788